T0266737

Advance Praise for
Awake with Asashoryu

"The essayist Elisabeth McKetta is a wonderful story-teller who takes us generously into her life, which always seems initially off-balance, full of falls, disappointments, and reversals, and yet, in the end, joyous. Her collection is humane, amusing, touching, and very satisfying."

—**Phillip Lopate**, author of *To Show and to Tell: The Craft of Literary Nonfiction*

"Captivating and evocative and original."

—**Grace Dane Mazur**, author of *The Garden Party*

"In eleven essays that are at once intricate and expansive, Elisabeth Sharp McKetta examines the work of becoming oneself through the battle between the longing for travel and the desire for home. At the heart of this remarkable memoir-in-essays is the wisdom of all fairytales: the taming of wildness that must happen in order for us to survive. The book is partly about grief for what must be lost in the process: romance or friendship that is outgrown or broken, homes that are made and abandoned. But equally important are the moments that turn domesticity and compromise into unexpected gifts: a hedgehog that appears from a hole in the wall and is restored; a burden from a mother-daughter conflict that—in another time and place—is transformed into a favorite garment. *Awake with Asashoryu* is a lyrical book about learning to live in kindness and beauty."

—**Kyoko Mori**, author of *The Dream of Water* and *Shizuko's Daughter*

"Elisabeth McKetta's essay collection, a self-described 'moebius strip of endless minutes,' is a dreamy, sensitive account of the many different kinds of love that beset us over a lifetime: the love of daughters for fathers, of mothers for children, of dog-owners for their dogs. McKetta's rich imagination and febrile sensibility are well-matched by her passion for fairy tales with their strange, ambiguous fusions of light and dark. A ruminative account of one woman's journey to adulthood, *Awake with Asashoryu* is a both a lovely and a provocative book."

   —**Christina Thompson**, Editor, *Harvard Review*

"Elisabeth Sharp McKetta pushes at the fabric encasing the relationships and passions of the people around her and dreams about what kind of life to live. Brimming with wisdom and humor, *Awake with Asashoryu* allows the reader's understanding to grow along with the writer in this remarkable book."

   —**Lynn C. Miller**, author of *The Unmasking*
      and *The Day After Death*

"A shimmering first essay collection from a gifted and skilled writer."

   —**Kim Cross**, author of *What Stands in a Storm*

"A mythical and graceful voice."

   —**Nancy Sommers**, Harvard lecturer and essayist

"Reading Elisabeth Sharp McKetta is like diving into a dark blue universe."

   —**Anna Ospelt**, translator and author of the
      German books *Sammelglück* and *Wurzelstudien*

Praise for
Elisabeth Sharp McKetta's
Other Books

"The imaginative reworking of the mythology of death and the afterlife creates a remarkable mode for examining love and loss. McKetta uses language with an artistry that evokes sensory experience . . . The quality of suspended reality is beautifully apt for a tale focused on and inspired by water, the ocean, and swimming, and for McKetta's thematic progression from suffering to awareness, acceptance, and transcendence."

    —*Booklist* on *She Never Told Me About the Ocean*

"I've always admired the writing of Elisabeth Sharp McKetta, and her beautiful, ambitious first novel demonstrates why . . . She has offered us a complicated portrait of mothers and daughters, cupped inside one another like nesting dolls."

    —**Arthur Golden**, author of *Memoirs of a Geisha*,
      on *She Never Told Me About the Ocean*

"A tidal and intimate book, brimming over with wonders and terrors and the watery echoes that bind generations of women. What a pleasure this book is from start to finish."

    —**Karen Russell**, author of *Swamplandia!*,
      on *She Never Told Me About the Ocean*

"When someone is ill, many old cultures say that they have lost their story. I believe that reading the stories in *What Doesn't Kill Her* will help each of us to trust and tell our own."

—**Gloria Steinem**, on *What Doesn't Kill Her*

"For some years now, I have been reading and appreciating Elisabeth Sharp McKetta's exceptional Poetry for Strangers project. With generosity, inclusiveness, and openness to the wonders of nature and the human spirit, McKetta reaches out to those strangers, encountered by chance, inviting them to participate in an art form that non-writers so often consider alien territory. She is a bridge-builder of the most original kind. And, equally admirable, from this unpredictable starting point she writes many amazingly good, complexly developed poems, imbued with her own intelligence, wit, and kind perceptiveness."

—**Lydia Davis**, author of *Can't and Won't* and
    Essays One, on *Poetry for Strangers*

"Elisabeth McKetta taps fairy tales, and, presto, they transform themselves into living things that reach out and tug at us, reminding us of the exquisite fragility in 'once upon a time.'"

—**Maria Tatar**, Harvard Professor and author of
    The Fairest of Them All: Snow White and *21 Tales
    of Mothers and Daughters*, on *The Fairy Tales
    Mammals Tell*

"Elisabeth McKetta grapples with the bedrock basics of being human. All of the imperatives of flesh—love, lust, the making and breaking of hearts, marriage, children, and all the rest—get full play in her writing."

—**Ben Fountain**, author of *Brief Encounters with
    Che Guevara*, on *The Fairy Tales Mammals Tell*

AWAKE

with

ASASHORYU

AWAKE

with

ASASHORYU

and Other Essays

ELISABETH SHARP McKETTA

PAUL DRY BOOKS
Philadelphia 2022

First Paul Dry Books Edition, 2022

Paul Dry Books, Inc.
Philadelphia, Pennsylvania
www.pauldrybooks.com

ISBN: 978-1-58988-166-2

Printed in the United States of America

Library of Congress Control Number: 2022936140

To my parents

Contents

Author's Note

I CAME TO MEMOIR at the same time I came to fairy tales, just before I turned twenty. This collision sparked the writer that I would become, and so it makes sense somehow that each of my personal essays would have a fairy tale or myth—or some very old story—at its heart. If you look closely, you can find them.

What genre is this? It could be coming of age, for the essays dance like wayward princesses around the question of how to grow up without losing oneself. I think of them as mythic memoir (or depending on the day, asymptotic autobiography). More simply, they are stories from my life, mostly true.

AWAKE

with

ASASHORYU

Awake with Asashoryu

1

I am awake.

A siren woke me and now I can't get back to sleep. So now I'm sitting up in the dark and stroking my sleeping dog, who has come home for Christmas with me. I can tell from the way her legs flicker that she is dreaming of chasing something.

I do what I always do when awake at my childhood house: go find my father. This night, I find him in the study, sitting on the green plaid chair and watching the computer.

"Lizzie!" he cries, happy that someone else is awake with him in the early morning. "You're just in time to see sumo. Come sit. Do you want coffee?" He ushers me into the chair where he has been sitting, fills me a mug from the French press, and then stands behind me, fidgeting. He drinks coffee all day and all night and his hands shake from it. He could never be a surgeon. But he would probably never want to be. In this way I differ from my father: He *is* something, in his case an attorney and a dad, and he is content being so. I fear being anything, ever, because it might keep me from being all the other things I might one day want to be.

What I see on the computer screen surprises me: two enormous Japanese men with hair tucked into puffy brioche-like buns slamming into each other. It takes me a long time to realize that none of the commentary is in English.

"Dad," I ask, "how do you understand what's happening?"

"If you see enough sumo you begin to get things straight. Looky here. Watch what happens." One of the men is bowing around a circle, his diaper-thong-loincloth riding straight up the crack of his colossal buttocks. I am embarrassed to be awake with my dad in the middle of the night, watching obese mostly-naked men wrestle.

But it is clear that my dad doesn't mind at all. He has begun narrating: "Look at how the winner helps his opponent up. Now he's bowing—that's tradition . . ." From the speakers I hear applause getting louder and louder, and I ask who all the people are cheering for. "Pay attention here," he says. "All the noise is because Asashoryu is in the next match."

Rewind.

Twenty years earlier, in the same house, I am awake: I am five years old and awake in the early morning with my dad. He reads the paper, I rest on the sofa and look up at the ceiling, spying a cockroach directly above me. I already know a few things about cockroaches from school: they do not have brains, but basal ganglia. This is why they can live partially smushed. Their only imperative is to stay alive, to win the civilization race.

"Dad," I ask. "Will it fall on me?"

"Of course not," he says, and that minute it does. As if it heard and let go.

I want to tell my father this: Although you are not immortal like the cockroaches, you are at least in better shape than the sumo wrestlers. But I do not say this. Certain things are better to say to yourself than to your dad. Instead, I kiss him on the forehead and go back to bed.

2

Remember those mornings, Girl. Remember them, and one day you'll sing them back to yourself like that Hamelin piper sang his past to those rats. Soon your nights will have their own sleepwalking. Soon you will have a daughter and will wake each night in stark panic, dreaming of losing her. You will trace paths through your house, milk-full and awake at night, in the early morning, in the dark dad-hours when Asashoryu wrestles.

Your dad will lose his mother in February, exactly a month after you give birth to a daughter. And it is sort of a transfer of souls, isn't it, between an infant girl and a dying woman who share the same genes? Will they high-five on their ways in and out?

So remember how (once upon a time at your childhood house) you were a daughter, just a daughter. You were so much somebody's daughter, with your old bedroom and your dog trailing behind your every step. You were your sleepless father's daughter.

3

This is who fathers are in fairy tales: the kings who protect their daughters from having any sort of fun. One king hires soldiers to spy on his daughters (all twelve of them!) by tracking them down to a secret lair where they dance all night, ravaging their shoes, a habit that depletes their father's purse even more than any of their other princess habits. That king, as a reward for this information, forces his eldest daughter to marry the soldier-snoop, as if she were her father's currency.

Or else fathers are humble peasant men who build fences and beds and who fetch lettuces, rampion, arugula, and rapunzel for their pregnant wives, doddering into the wrong garden and being forced, by a witch cleverer than he, to make a trade for the produce: his daughter, perhaps.

And in "Beauty and the Beast," the man loses his daughter again. He can give up his life to the Beast or he can give up his daughter's life, and when the daughter is quicker on the draw, the father shrugs as if to say, *Well, I'll get the check next time.*

My father is like none of these men.

In fairy tales, fathers get that daughters are tricky—we traffic in half-truths. Sons will say what they mean and tell you where they're going. You might tell them not to go and they'll go anyway, but at least they'll tell you. But daughters are made up of secrets. And it is a father's job to crack those secrets. For the girls' own good, of course.

But what if it is the other way around?

4

When I return to my parents' house for the Christmas holidays, it becomes clear to me that my father never sleeps. Not really. He falls asleep against his will in the early evenings but then throttles awake throughout the night, wrestling with his work, with himself, or with whatever questions plague men after midnight. He always wakes by two a.m. This is convenient, because the sumo tournaments take place at that time, and my father can watch them live on the computer. The matches flicker in the night, lasting on average a few seconds, a minute at most. He goes downtown to his office at six, seven a.m., and what he does in between sumo and work, I have no idea. Works the crosswords. Naps. Munches on popcorn. Watches Asashoryu rise to the top of the charts.

My father likes many things about Asashoryu: his discipline and skill, and also his name, which translates to "Blue Dragon of the Morning," and which has that strange sound "ryu" at the end, giving whiplash to an American tongue. I think my father also likes that Asashoryu is an outsider, Mongolian in a Japanese sport, and yet he keeps winning. He is a prodigy of sorts: at age twenty-three, Asashoryu became a *yokozuna*, the highest rank in sumo.

But what my father likes most about Asashoryu is his reputation as sumo's bad boy. In 2003, Asashoryu is scolded and disqualified from a match because he pulled an opponent's topknot like a boy pulling a girl's pigtails to get attention in school. It was a childish move, but he was a child. In 2007, Asashoryu is suspended from competing because he got spotted playing soccer when he was supposed to be resting from an injury—the first time in sumo's two thousand-year history that a *yokozuna* is suspended.

"Mongolian liar!" headlines scream. "Asa Scoundrel," websites pun. "*Maketa*," cartoon bubbles have him admit: "I fucked up, I lose," from the Japanese word *makeru*, to fuck up. *Maketa* is past tense. We, incidentally, are McKettas.

My dad is at once thrilled and appalled at Asashoryu's suspension. My father would never have made such a JV move. But Asashoryu is in his twenties and my father is older, and who knows what my father would have done at Asashoryu's age? At my age. Asashoryu takes risks my father never would have chanced. Asashoryu will have peaked in his twenties, while my father is chugging uphill slowly, conserving energy, and poised to live a long, long time.

Why he became interested in sumo mystifies me.

Why *I* became interested in his interest in sumo is even less clear to me.

I played sports in high school but have never liked watching them. I sleep through the night. But in the days leading up to Christmas, I find myself napping during the afternoons and staying awake at night with Dad and Asashoryu.

5

My father drove a taxi when he was a young man. His college degree prepared him to become a mathematics professor, but he graduated during the Vietnam War, and so he drove a cab while he waited to be drafted.

The war ended. A year later, with his draft number burned forever into his mind, he found a high school that needed a math teacher and he lived on campus for three years, drawing Euclidian figures on chalkboards and saving up money. On campus, you spend nothing—you have food, shelter, toilet paper, and your weekends are pre-subscribed to dorm duty. My father lived in the dorm and got along very well with the boys, as he knew a great deal about M*A*S*H, which the boys watched, and he pretended not to recognize the smell of marijuana, which the boys smoked.

I know all this.

I know this too: After college, but before teaching, my father wrote in a letter to his own father that he was not going to get a job teaching math or going to law school or battling his way through academia, or doing any of the other tasks for which his degree had prepared him. Instead he wanted to wander and test his skills to survive.

My twenty-one-year-old father wrote: "If I don't do it now, I will never know. Your survival was tested growing up, and you know. But my brothers and I have never had to take that risk. Now I want to do it."

His Ukrainian-descended father, once a nineteen-year-old coal miner, now a middle-aged scientist, scoffed. "What is the point of suffering," he wrote back sensibly, "when your mother and I worked this hard to make a life that would keep you three boys safe and out of suffering? We did the suffering for you. Now your generation has evolved past it. *Get a job, Mike*," he said, and the conversation ended.

After teaching, but before I was born, my father moved on to law. Yet when I imagine him in those days, before he had a daughter, I see him driving strangers through city streets, spinning the wheels in his eternal taxi. I imagine a ferry-conductor, a raft man. A pathmaker who tamed himself before I existed. He is a man of great presence, and yet I see him in the great silence of fatherhood.

I decide, in my twenties, that I wish to understand my father better. So I visit Washington, D.C., where he lived fresh out of law school, his hair still exuberantly red, his book pages still starchy. I visit the bakeries where he lunched, sampling the sandwiches he described. I stand in the snow at the base of his old driveway, which twists like a cartoon villain's beard down the suburban hillside. The window-shades are drawn, so no wrong figures can replace the life that I have compiled and imposed upon this small gray frame. A light turns on upstairs.

I walk downtown, near the office where he worked, the home of his first job at a desk. I wonder: How will he think of himself as he ages, how will he characterize the "him" in his life? As a young father, newly married? Or a math teacher, trying to get high school potheads to care about numbers? Or a mischievous teenager with a pocket full of chocolate slipped to him by his mother to sustain him through church?

I search his local library, the empty lot where his bank used to be, the houses of several friends. I search the park where he took me as a child, pausing to wait for him on the swings. I try to look up his old lovers to give me some sense of him as he had been, but the only one I find is my mother.

At evening I leave my undertaking, tired and with aching feet. I turn a corner and read a map, wishing for a place to rest. I decide to look in one final place: in the cemetery. My father has always admired the austere beauty of graves. Graveyards are great places to walk, with their short, reverently clipped grass, and my father dearly loves to walk. When my sisters and I were children, he took us to cemeteries to make grave-rubbings. I start to enter the gates but cannot. Now, as an adult, I fear the silence that wafts among the dead.

So I stand on the curb and raise my hand for a taxi.

Few taxis are out, but across the street one stops. I see the silhouette of the driver; as he rolls the window down, I make out the bright red hair of a very young man.

The driver doesn't call to ask where I am going, and I don't tell him. He watches me for a long moment, and I know that he recognizes me. My crossing light is not green, and he shakes his head.

I run for him anyway. I need to see him closely, to know his voice and to see that he's happy.

I wave my hands so that he will understand what I want. So that he will wait.

He winks, and keeps driving.

6

During the holidays when there is nobody at his office, my father is at a loss for what to do. One morning after Christmas I have some errands to run: I need a book for school, a new toothbrush, a costume for a New Year's Eve party. I invite my father and he gladly accepts and the errands become a full-day affair that includes a drive to a landfill and a stop at a barbeque restaurant whose kitchen smokes and flames and reminds me of hell.

At the restaurant my father over-orders and we take four pounds of meat home to feed the dogs. At the costume shop he buys several Mardi Gras masks. At Walmart he buys a four-foot squishy magenta caterpillar. It has happy plastic eyes and curlicue plastic eyelashes and a stitched-on smile. He buys some artificial rose petals, too. He buys and buys and buys. When we arrive back home, he gives my mom the caterpillar and tosses a handful of the fake rose petals on the living room floor.

"Mike," my mom says warningly, as the dogs begin to lick the petals. My father shrugs and picks them up and puts them back into the bag. Before going to bed, I spy the pink caterpillar in the laundry room. It has been squished on top of the cabinets, in the plastic crates with the dogs' toys.

That night, I stay awake until dawn on the phone with the man who will become my husband. I tell him about the caterpillar and for some reason I almost begin to cry. My phone battery runs out and cuts us off. The next morning I receive a voice message from him, saying he does not hate it when my phone cut us off, not at all, but instead he loves that we'd rather keep on talking and risk the cut-off, than lose whatever seconds we might have left.

7

There is an overbelly and an underbelly to all fathers: the overbelly is his marriage to my mother, his four children, his house behind a gate, his line of black and navy suits that he wears each day to the office. The underbelly is that he separates his black and navy socks into opposite parts of his sock-drawer and gets flustered if anybody mixes them up. The underbelly is that he hides chocolate candy in his sock drawer; the day I learned this was the same day I learned not to mix up his socks.

The overbelly is his facility with numbers, the infinite city maps he keeps in his head, the fact that he always, always, always wins at cards, even though I have never known him to initiate a card game. The underbelly is his sleeplessness, how his nights last forever and he fills them with sumo, and how he bites his nails when he is nervous before trial or on the way to the airport.

His smile is both over- and underbelly.

So is his punctuality. It is overbelly in that he is always the first to arrive for meetings and events. It is underbelly in that the day of my wedding, my father and I drove together and got caught in traffic, and my father panicked at the thought that we might be late. And then what? I wondered. What wedding starts without the bride?

It is underbelly that he does not eat when my mother is out of town; or he eats, but only hard-boiled eggs, labeled in a plastic bowl in the refrigerator, and pre-popped popcorn from a bag. He drinks coffee from a French press. The pomegranate seeds of his underworld are few and unnourishing, but somehow they sustain him.

It is overbelly that he makes a lot of money, and overbelly too that he spends it in excess. But it is underbelly that money means little to him, which is why he always has too much. Money, for him, is something to shed: an ugly, guilty thing that is best given away.

Sumo swells one belly into the other. Once I am asked in an elevator in the town where I grew up, in a building near the building where my dad works downtown, if it is true that my dad has begun sumo-wrestling.

It is true and it is not true.

8

To become a sumo wrestler, you must fill your belly with beer and rice, starting when you are young, so that by adulthood your stomach will have stretched to accommodate all the food you will need. In sumo, the body is master, not the mind. The only just comparison is a pregnant woman, first trimester, when the alien enters and needs to eat.

Like horses, sumo wrestlers live in *heya*, training stables; and also like horses, they are fed, dressed, exercised according to a traditional code that will help them win. They wake early, at five a.m., to exercise and fast—they fast for hours so that by the time they eat lunch, their body is in fat-storing starvation mode. For their two daily meals, sumo wrestlers eat *chankonabe*, single-pot soups of fish, meat, and vegetables, and they eat bowl after bowl of rice until they cannot hold anymore. Then they nap, so the calories will quickly become fat.

Like horses, their manes are ceremoniously tended. Simply to fix a sumo wrestler's hair requires a ten-year apprenticeship. When a sumo career ends, the wrestler must sacrifice his hair; his topknot is cut off in a ritual inside the sumo ring. Depending on the wrestler, over two hundred people may have the privilege of cutting off a strand of the great wrestler's mane before the stable-master makes the final cut.

Like horses, these wrestlers are bred for sport, father to father to father.

I am beginning to think about fatherhood, how it is impossible to comprehend fatherhood in a spouse without first deferring back to one's own dad. Until I met my husband, it was impossible for me to comprehend loving a man who did not closely resemble my father. Now, it's impossible to comprehend loving something enough to not-sleep for it.

This will change.

9

In the middle of the night, I sort through the clutter of my life at my parents' house, winnowing down to the few things I will take when I move. I have finished school and it is time to go. I have a mind full of manuscripts, and a belly distending not with beer and rice but with new life.

My father walks past my room while I am packing my books. His thin mouth frowns with wrinkles and exhaustion. I follow him into the kitchen. He sets a stack of mail on the kitchen counter and turns to make coffee, and in doing so his elbow knocks all the mail onto the floor. I help him pick it up. The tired look hasn't gone from his eyes, but he is smiling again.

He says, "Lizzie, take care never to be really good at what you do, because it means that you're never done."

I say that I will do my best.

"Are you having a happy life?" he asks.

"I am," I say, and I mean it. "Are you?"

"Oh," he says, with a deep laugh, "Very happy. I have had such a blessed, happy life, been so lucky with my family, in this job I love, working with such honorable colleagues. So lucky. I hope you are this lucky."

"So do I," I say. Then I ask, "How was your day today?"

"So busy. And tomorrow will be busier, and Friday, too. But," he says, reaching into his shirt pocket, "here is some disappointing news."

I unfold the piece of paper he hands me. It is a spreadsheet, created on Excel and filled in with my father's crabbed, geometric handwriting. On the left, vertical, are sumo wrestlers' names, along with their age, height, weight, country of origin, rank. Horizontally across the top are their names again, and my dad has filled in the results of each match in the squares where names meet.

"Asashoryu lost," Dad says. "Now he's tied for second with nine other people."

"Who beat him?"

"A man named Hakuho."

"An old-timer?"

"No, very young, but already a *yokozuna*. He just became one, at age twenty-two. Asa is no longer the only *yokozuna*."

He gives me a kiss and says that he is getting up in two hours and heads off to his bedroom. The door thuds behind him. My dog looks confused. She has been following me from room to room, as if I were trying to trick her by sleeping somewhere else. It is hours past her bedtime.

10

My father worries about failure to do his duty, and I worry about sleepwalking through life and missing things. My father listens and always says the correct things. I listen as well as I can, but then I slip and ask the sort of questions that poke holes like a twig fiddling a sweater, and I look for things to unravel.

What we share, my father and I, is that we both want something that lies eternally outside the halo of our grasp—whereas most other successful adults I know act as if they already have gotten everything they ever wanted: a job and a family and freedom and security. Most adults, at my father's age, may rest fatly on their laurels, top roosters in the small coop they have carved out of the world.

But not my father.

Men like my father are either silent and wish to speak; roguish and wish to settle; settled and wish for freedom; overfed and wish for the scrappiness and hunger of their twenties. Any way you frame it, these men want. Want is something I can understand. Desire involves something unraveling in a corner, and being a writer involves always having something unraveling in a corner. When I watch my father watch sumo, I wonder what it is, exactly, that he wants from his life.

My father loves maps, math, art, wine, and sumo. He loves gushing about his wife and holding people's babies. He loves his family, and to support them he works full-time, overtime, out of town for weeks at a time. My father taught me about achievement and commitment and love, but I grew up interested only in love. Love and writing. And I knew, always, that writing is really only a way to love the world full-time.

In my late twenties I was perched and ready to fly, moving from the city of my childhood into a new city, a new decade. My dreams were shifting, lightening: I had shed the heavy sleep, the dreams of myself as a precarious block in a towering legacy where I could fall in fear and disappoint the father I loved. I could fuck up. *Maketa! Maketa!* Like Asa Scoundrel, but without ever having peaked. I told myself sternly: you have a choice. Figure out what you want from life, and either stay asleep to it, or wake yourself up.

So I ran through the security gates of thirty, and the metal detectors caught my steely poison dreams and forbade me from carrying them through. What I carried instead were my dog, and my husband, and my husband's dog, and my laptop filled with twelve years worth of stories. A few black dresses. A teapot, a library card. A small collection of expensive hats bought for me by my father.

11

In a kingdom across the sea, Asashoryu steps down. He is no longer a *yokozuna* because he got in trouble again, for beating up a waiter again, and the only honorable thing to do is leave the sport where he has ruled for seven years. This is better than seppuku but the same principle. He will play soccer uncurbed; he will be paid to advertise products that are being promoted on sandwich boards at the sumo matches of wrestlers that once he easily dominated. Nearly four hundred people will have the honor of cutting his topknot.

My father has fallen asleep. In the middle of the night, there is the television, shining, noctilucent, and my father snoring on the green carpet on the study floor—the room, incidentally, where my mother's dogs discovered that the carpet was the same color as grass. The poo-room, my husband called it once.

My husband wakes earlier and earlier.

My baby shifts and hums all night, waking me.

My father catches a snore in his throat. He will stop breathing eventually. They all will. Hard to imagine at age thirty that one day I will, too.

The parade of sumo will go on for centuries, men in diapers training like horses in stables; new rulers rise and will fall, for those who are awake to watch. The sun goes down earlier and earlier, lengthening night into something intolerable.

The twelve dancing princesses get caught by their father.

I am awake.

Robber Face

WHEN I WAS a child I read a fairy tale about a robber who wished to marry a well-bred girl. He knew nobody would take him with his robber's face, so he used stolen money to have a mask made—a perfect face, virtuous and innocent and trustworthy. With his mask he courted the girl and she fell for him. They wed. They bred. And many years into their life together, he confessed his story. He was only pretending to be good. He had a mask. "Take it off, then," his wife said. He did—and the face below matched the mask exactly.

GROWING UP in a family of four kids, a lawyer dad who traveled, and a PhD-ed and law-degreed mom who chose to stay home with her young, I spent most of my time in the company of a crowd. The exceptions were those days after school when I went over to my nana's apartment and had a woman all to myself. My nana was partially deaf, a heavy smoker and heavier drinker, and a reader who could float on her back in a swimming pool while reading a book. We adored each other.

We cooked, read, talked, and she gave me boxes of her old sewing scraps, corralled in a Cutty Sark Scotch Whisky box.

When she was dying of liver failure at age sixty-seven, everybody who came through her hospital room believed she would recover. Each time she disagreed—in her quiet reader's voice, laden, I imagine, with subtlety and symbolism—the room silenced for a moment and then all the well-meaning adult voices swelled up to interrupt her, to say, *stop talking doom, you will be fine, you will kick this liver thing.*

In the end, she chose me, age nine, as the one she trusted not to argue. The room had emptied for a brief time—the adults were in the hall—and I was alone with her, and she held hard onto my hands and peered hard into my eyes, squinting at the brightness outside the window: it was springtime in Texas. "Elisabeth," she said, drawing out each syllable in my name, "I am going to die."

I did not interrupt her as the adults had done. What I did was worse. I ran screaming down the hospital hallway looking for another adult. I was whisked away home; she was told by the adults once more that she would be just fine; and late that night, she died.

It was the first time a person I loved had trusted me and I had let her down. It would not be the last.

No MATTER what else the adults told me afterward, I knew the truth: my woman was alone at the end, grasping for connection—and if this could happen to her, then it seemed the human condition is to be alone and grasping for others. This knowledge panicked me. It isolated me, too.

It is easy to say now that the fairy tales of religion, which my Episcopalian elementary school taught us each day in chapel, appealed to my imagination and to the writer I would become. But in the two and a half years following this first breach of life by death, I descended into a bizarre stage of religiosity. *He descended into hell . . . He ascended into heaven . . .* These prayers we said each morning were nonsense, as far as my heathen parents were concerned.

I was alive when the Challenger blew; I watched it on TV. I knew that humans went into the sky, somewhere, and I also knew that there was an alternative to flight, and that was fire. The death of my most treasured adult, the one I felt so possessive of and singularly heard by, even though I had failed to hear her, merged in my mind with heaven, hell, outer space, and the people who died there. I became, in a whirl of weeks, obsessed with the afterlife. Obsessed, specifically, with a terrible idea that I might go to heaven, where prayers promised entry to believers like me, and that my parents, nonbelievers, would go to hell.

My choices: heaven alone, or hell with my family. Both alternatives frankly sucked. This paradox ran through my head day and night. It merged with the sort of detail-obsessed superstition many kids have (don't step on a crack, you'll break your mother's back) and I found myself saying silently, *step on that crack, you'll go to heaven, step on that crack, hell.* Every single day of being alive was terrifying. But being dead wasn't any better, for then the theoretical choice would become actual.

Fifth and sixth grade were marked by this mania. I dared tell nobody, because somehow I felt sworn to secrecy, a heaven-hell-determining oath between myself and presumably God, or Nana, or whoever was waiting for me on the other side. But my family knew. They knew because they'd find me kneeling in prayer in the kitchen and doing other strange and unsanctioned things. But I refused to talk. Once they tried to get me to talk to the one believer in my family, my Catholic aunt; she told me her own stories of trying to do well by God, such as not looking in a mirror for a year. This was well-meant but did not help. Everything I did, every wrong word, every wrong thought, every wrong action, every mischief—such as going to toilet-paper some cute boy's house with my elementary school friends—glowed in my mind as a sin. I spent my days heavy with the awareness of my death and all the loneliness that would follow it.

By the summer before seventh grade, I had worn myself out. I think some part of my brain dedicated to my survival told me that God or no, heaven or hell or only blessed earth, I had better let go of worrying about this stuff if I wanted to make it to adulthood. So I did.

I couldn't control what happened after I died— maybe I was good, maybe I wasn't, maybe none of us were, maybe goodness in general was simply a collective mask—but I could act on the loneliness front while I was alive. I knew this was, to some extent, a sham. I had seen first-hand that you could love someone completely and still run screaming from them as they lay dying. Death, it seemed, was the only story. All the other stuff in life—friendship, fun, toilet-papering and whatnot—however lovely, would not last. Those were only temporary distractions from the eternal question.

Still, needing that distraction, I turned toward action. I decided to screw my energy to the sticking point and be very, very kind to everybody. If somebody needed a friend, I would include her. I put a great deal of effort into this, and my way of doing so at age twelve was to be very goofy, very giggly, very innocent-seeming, and very hyper. Look up hyper hypo in the old Saturday Night Lives and you'll get something of an idea of what I was like. My efforts worked and I was not lonely at school.

Yet my isolation stayed around me, like a ghost sheet. The true self, with its knowledge and its fears—this I could not reveal to any of my friends. But I had company and people who valued me, both at school and at home, and this was something. Movies helped: watching movies and entering another story alongside other people. This bonded me to other lives. I thought less about heaven and hell—except for those nights when we all went toilet papering, then I felt reminded of my sinner's guilt.

THE SUMMER between seventh and eighth grade I learned another way to leave your death awareness behind, briefly, and connect to another person: kissing. My first kiss was a sordid affair, in a broom closet at a condominium at the beach. My second kiss didn't count; it was supposed to be from my boyfriend on my thirteenth birthday, but instead ended up being a wet peck on the lips from his dad in an exuberant embarrassing dad-swoop in front of both our families. Years later I wrote a poem about it called "The Wrong Kiss." My real second kiss was finally this boyfriend, though a few weeks later. My third kiss, post-boyfriend, was the best of all, but I couldn't tell anyone. It happened at a family lake camp. The boy was not a boy at all but a twenty-something man who taught waterskiing. My body had matured beyond my age while his had not kept up, an illusion that made us appear closer in age, though we both suspected a wide gap. We kissed—and nothing more—in his Texas pickup truck. For the rest of the night, I could not hide my rapturous smile, reflecting to me in the mirror. Perhaps there was a second story, besides death: perhaps love, even temporary love, was worthwhile.

I went back to school in September after this marvelous summer of kisses. I had told nobody about any of them, but the boyfriend (by this point former boyfriend) spread the news of our kiss far and wide, and the story grew and grew. On my first day of eighth grade, I went from being the girl who was everybody's friend, formerly the girl who was afraid to step on hellcracks, to the girl who the boys and even some girls called a "horny ho." Boys who I didn't know grabbed at my breasts in the hallway, stared at me licking their lips suggestively across the classroom, stuck fingers without invitation down my jean shorts. They called out at recess, *you are so ugly, you are so horny, you are just a ho.*

The old crisis began to swell again. There would not be salvation for me in prayer and belief and being as good as possible, nor would there be salvation in physical intimacy, in being a jolly sinner here on earth—one was too private, the other too public, and both horribly shameful. My friends were not much help: they too felt afraid of being left out, though I suspect their terror was about social groups, while mine was about the afterlife—but in the end, it didn't matter. One group of girls in my grade pushed me against a bathroom wall at a birthday party and demanded that I swear on the Bible that I had not done all of these things I had been accused of. The religious fear lingered enough—I would not swear—and I survived eighth grade, tainted in this way.

I went to a different high school—went on and learned, and focused on friends, though even with my closest friends I always kept one part of my heart private, unconnected, one part that nobody could see—a secret protection, like a layer of fat for the winter, or a candle at an altar. I never got into drugs, I think primarily because I was afraid of what my mind might reveal if I dug too deeply beneath its rational floorboards. I played sports and for the most part I enjoyed schoolwork—I did well in high school—I excelled in field hockey—I got into Harvard—and I went to college a virgin, because hell if anyone would have any reason ever again to call me horny ho.

As THE YEARS parted like water, I found people—slowly, and one at a time—with whom I could share my solitude. From age twenty onward, I claimed writing as something I enjoyed and was good at, and through it I slowly hauled myself above ground. I began to connect myself to the other selves in the world. I found a joy, a lightness, a grounding in the world of the living, on good days. Most days, eventually, grew to be good. Eventually, I wove a life around this forbidden knowledge, as muscle forms stronger around an injured ligament. Yes, underlying life there is loneliness, a grasping for connection.

But still.

But still, I could make my life about forging connections. I could become a writer to connect through words; a teacher to connect through ideas; a mother and a spouse to connect through biology and love. I would disappoint more people, but I would also do well by others. I would be called beautiful. The taboos and terrors of my childhood would melt into adult routine.

I still surround myself with a quietness: mornings of solitude when I am alone, writing, while my husband and babies sleep like the dead. Sometimes I wonder if this is the right way, or if somehow my heart is too closed, and I need to find a way to wrench it open more to chaos, to mystery.

I would grow up to study fairy tales, and when my children, growing up in Idaho, which is about a third Latter Day Saints, would ask me about God, I would tell them about myths and fairy tales and even Bible stories, to the extent that I remember them. I tell them stories about my childhood, about my nana, too, and I try to offer them the depth of attention she gave me. It feels as if my babies are grounded in the real, much more so than I ever was. They are connected to each other, to their dad and to me and their friends, and they are not ashamed to talk about big things; they seem unafraid. We talk at home about birth, love, sex, death, and any question that they ask. This feels right.

And I have found, in adulthood, that there are other stories besides death. Two, to be specific. Birth and love. Those three stories—birth, love, and death—cycle through our lifespan in a thousand different ways, many unseen, many times in a single day. I could spend my adulthood recognizing this holy trinity, rather than only seeing death.

My young believe that I am good but not perfect. Once in a while, they sense a vulnerability in me, and they come, usually offering a stuffed animal like a holy gift, to offer comfort. There are days when I wonder whether the mask has become real after all these years. I am taken back to the original petrifying question: *Am I good? Am I only pretending to be good?*

So the mask, it seemed, was a way to cover imperfect love with perfect love. Maybe this is what we all do, and in the way that green things grow toward the sun, perhaps our life's work is to grow toward the mask. To grow and grow, until finally our real face becomes our ideal face and the robber mask pops off and is gone.

The Softness of Spikes

As I approached age twenty, I had an imaginary version of myself who made me nervous: her name was Luba, and she was who I might become if I let go of myself in every possible way.

Once upon a time, Luba looked like me, but now she is nearly three hundred pounds. She has no edges anymore, no curves or shape. She understands the world only so far as people look and act like her. She loves to play judge: to Luba, most of the world's young women (myself included) are heathens, wild girl-libertines with too-fierce ambitions and too many boyfriends. She looks like the status quo breaded and fried and powdered with sugar, wrapped in pink and delivered for Valentine's Day. In my imaginings, Luba settled in marriage for Jasper, a widower who is prematurely gray and beefy; he has a mean streak, but most people consider him jolly. A bit in the vein of an off-season Santa Claus.

My Luba is a stepmother to Jasper's patiently sweet son Samuel, on whom she lavishes attention. When

Samuel is of dating age, Luba sneaks around after him at night, parking a few hundred feet back to see where he is and with whom. She would probably read his diary, if he kept one.

My imaginary scenarios get worse and worse when Samuel is around. I don't think Luba should be allowed around children, a mean thought that would surely break her corseted heart, for children are what Luba lives for—infants, biting terriers, spied-upon stepsons. But she never had children of her own. Instead, Luba has dogs, and Luba's dogs hate children, and indeed Samuel has many scars from Luba's dogs' bites. Luba never trains them. Rather than setting any rules, she just crosses her fingers, pours out her whole heart, and hopes, loves, fears. For all Luba's abundant softness, her dogs are nothing but sharp nerves and teeth.

Like the flashbacks in a horror film, I keep having flashes of this woman, and interspersed with the grisly images of present-tense Luba are the vanished fossils of Luba before: when she had a moon-bright face and long legs. When her thin clothes washed over her like silky water over a mermaid. Surely as a younger woman she was a more fascinating, more glamorous, quicker, more daring version of me. She knew the music that would define each decade before anyone else her age did; she did everything, knew everyone, was free and wild and perfect; she sunbathed topless on European beaches, her long dark hair splayed across her pale breasts.

She dated high school seniors when she was an eighth grader, men in their twenties when she was a high school senior, and only when she was just about to graduate college did she bypass all the trifling events of her roaring twenties, all of the formal dances and first jobs of her friends, and decide to fall in love with Jasper—aged forty-two—and the idea of playing mother to his nearly-grown teenage son. Only then did my beautiful imagined alter ego spring forth into stepmotherhood, move out to the suburbs, and wilt.

Now, Luba loves to corner women alone and tell them all about her life together with her husband, of the romance of their honeymoon, and of how he used to carry her to bed. It is hard to imagine Jasper, with his cactus beard and his massive belly, carrying anyone to bed. It is hard to imagine him doing anything except sitting in his favorite black leather chair and making lewd jokes. He jokes about her weight, too; Luba winces but does not respond. What could she say?

Luba does not wear jewelry—her husband does not allow it. Jewelry is "for fancy women," Jasper says.

She does not wear sandals for the same reason.

Once upon a time, Luba had friends—but Jasper doesn't like for her to see them.

When a joke is made, he gets it and laughs. Then she laughs only once he's laughed first.

Whenever a question is asked of her, she looks at him to answer.

I want more children, Luba sometimes begs in bed at night. *I deserve more children.* But Jasper says he doesn't trust her genes enough for that.

Her household clutter is as irreducible as her body. Although she often complains about having too much stuff, she cannot bring herself to clean out their house or throw a single precious object away (and all of her objects are precious), so Samuel will have to do it when she and Jasper die. Her clutter moons about her, bulking up her hips, her house, and her purse, taking up more than her allotted space on earth.

The state of her life threatens me.

How could a woman grow into such a state? She has cultivated a milk-voice, spilling nothing but soft lactating praise, as if she were trying to breastfeed us all. She has become, literally, a boob. She emanates *Nurture, Nurture,* whereas we, the young, eye her with mutinous suspicion: we who are spiky and hard and ironic and smart. Even her name makes me squirm: Luba, like lube, slippery and ripe; rhyming with tuba, wet and hollow, descended from lyubov, Russian for love, too much love, too little discipline.

Every so often, I stopped to wonder: Who is Luba, and how did she come to live in my mind? Is she some sort of adult parable or human yield sign, standing silent and large at the guardrails as I sort out how will I become who I must become, and how will I avoid becoming who I must not become? Is she some sort of amalgamation of babysitters, aunts, sisters, friends— mashed up with some weak thing that lives inside me? She does not exist. I am not Luba, I am only Liz. She is all the ages at once, while I am only the age I am now. She has a stepson while I have only myself to care for.

So then what? What is she here to teach me?

THESE QUESTIONS lurked in my mind, taking her shape, as I warily approached adulthood. But when I was twenty, something happened that caused me to look at Luba—and love—in a new way.

I had acquired a pet hedgehog named Shimmie, and

it made me into a strange sort of nurturer. I loved her wet black-pearl nose, the smooth roundness of her perfect ears. If I had been safely redshirted on the sidelines of the maternal playing fields, having a small spiky mammal suddenly shoved me off the bench and into the game.

I watched her when she ate; I fed her bite by tiny bite, cutting soft things, cheese and dried apples, with a plastic picnic knife. I poured gerbil pellets into her food bowl and marveled at the crunching sound her long teeth made. She wouldn't have eaten those things in the wild, but it never occurred to me to investigate what she might have preferred. Shimmie lived in a covered cage in my dorm room, and I bored my friends with descriptions of how she wiped her small moist nose on my hand or how she stared, mesmerized, at the fire in the common room fireplace. I spent long evenings fascinated by watching her walk.

Suddenly I was captivated by mammalian impulses; I observed my secular self, floating over the milky, religious landscapes of motherhood.

In addition to a pet hedgehog, I also had a boyfriend, Carl. I loved him for three years, though I shrugged away before he could ask me to marry him. He softened me in ways I could not explain. For example, I stopped dressing up all of the time; instead of wearing short black dresses and red Texas boots, I slugged around in exercise clothes, because who was I trying to impress? I had already impressed him.

I began to look and feel older, a ma'am and no longer a miss. The first time a man called me ma'am, he was asking for money near my college dining hall. "Spare a dollar, ma'am?"

Ma'am? I looked down. I was wearing old yoga pants and a college sweatshirt, and those dorky Adidas slides that middle-aged women wear in locker rooms at the Y.

A further softening involved the matter of clutter. When Carl and I first were dating, he carried my three belongings in his pocket: an ID card, tinted chapstick, some money in a paper-clip. Then, several years in, I began carrying a purse. But not only a purse—a *mother*-purse, holding everything from chapstick to a camera to Tylenol, a notebook and mints that taste like violet, as well as band-aids, origami paper, a small silver tire gauge, a dozen pens, take-out menus. I knew this stage would come at some point, but still, when it happened I felt surprised.

When had I accrued such things?

I MANAGED to pack lightly when Carl and I traveled to London for two and a half weeks in the winter of our junior year of college—it was like a decadent pre-marriage honeymoon, though in a place that was far from tropical. He emptied his wardrobe of its footwear, and into his checked baggage went his weather-proof brown shoes, his running shoes, his second pair of running shoes, and, for nights when we would dress up for dinner, his nice brown shoes. I brought only my red boots that I wore on the plane. In the air, we did it in the airplane bathroom as a dare, drank some gin and tonics because on British Airways they are free, and then slept for the rest of the flight. When we arrived in the morning we went to the British Museum to get used to being awake. We were in good form. Carl joked mostly-seriously in the mummy room that the British explorers were all colonialist pirates who stole this stuff from Egypt. I joked less-seriously over an Indian food lunch that we should scour the hedges for a mate for Shimmie.

The winter daylight in Britain is short, lasting from breakfast-time until just before tea. We filled our short days and long nights with many things, including walks by the river, Indian food, sex, and ticking items off our *Let's Go!* travel guide. We pored over maps and memorized the Underground; we dressed in our best clothes (Carl in his nice brown shoes) and bought tickets for seats in *An Ideal Husband* and *Richard III*; we spent late nights listening to music in jazz bars around Sloane Square; we visited the Prime Meridian at Greenwich and kissed standing on opposite sides of the world; in the cold evenings we held hands inside an embarrassing red heart-shaped textile called a Smitten Mitten. We captured the whole trip on the video camera Carl had received for Christmas, and not one minute of it included anything having to do with hedgehogs.

The trip did include full English breakfast, however. The servers bustled in and out of the crowded tables with hot ceramic teapots and plates of eggs and sausage balanced on their bare arms. They were cheerful and chatty and called us all "Love." The hotel restaurant was crowded every morning, and usually we sat at a table only a few inches from the tables to either side.

One morning as I was sprinkling extra sugar in my tea, a gravelly-deep voice from a neighboring table caught my attention.

"You either shut up right now or go back to the room."

A silence followed. I was held rapt by the voice but was hesitant to look sideways. I stared hard at Carl's

toast, trying to watch from my peripheral vision without actually turning my head—a trick I play on myself
to feel as if I'm not eavesdropping. Who was this man
speaking to? Could it be a child, a parent? I sipped my
tea, my eyes still devouring the toast until Carl offered
me a piece. I shook my head. The man was American, I
could tell by his voice. Our waitress stopped at his table
to bring more juice, and I allowed my eyes to travel
first to her, then to him.

The voice came from a man, middle-aged and balding, and across from him was a woman of the same age,
wearing a yellow sweater and no lipstick, presumably
his wife. When the waitress asked him if he or his wife
needed anything, he smiled and said, "No, thank you."
As the waitress disappeared, the man's mouth pursed
into a scowl and he said something quietly—too quietly for me to hear—to the woman. She promptly left.
She said nothing; she just rose silently and obediently
and left. He sipped his tea.

Horrified, I turned to Carl. He met my eyes and
put his hands over mine.

"Did you see that?" I hissed.

"That was awful."

"That was—that was . . ." I fell silent, having no
words to articulate that this was cruelty, that this was
masculinity at its worst, that this was the language that
ruins women.

Carl supplied words. "That was sad and inappropri-
ate. How can a person speak to anyone else that way?"
He was speaking quietly, reminding me that I ought to
keep my voice down.

I, on the other hand, was fuming into a sputter.
"How can you speak to *your wife* that way? And how

can you then turn around and speak so nicely to the waitress?" At that moment the man interrupted by asking if he could please borrow our salt. Carl, always quick and polite, passed him both the salt and the pepper. The atrocious man thanked Carl and, to my further distress, winked at me.

The man left the restaurant soon after, and so did we. We were on our way to Paris for three days; Carl had reserved us Chunnel tickets and a hotel room. I fidgeted quietly during the cab ride to the station while Carl squeezed my hand reassuringly inside our Smitten Mitten. My hand was sweating and my mind's Rolodex was frantically flipping. I knew too many women who were in relationships like that; I could remember the early phone calls, the flowers and the visits, the elaborate acts of wooing. But a year or two in, the men had lost their early charm—there were more arguments, arguments that these young women tried to laugh over and ignore, but still the men always won. They were demanding, full of facts and logic, lacking in the safety nets of compromise or guilt or wonder, anything at all for the women, my joyful and independent friends and role models, to grasp and climb.

And I thought of my goofily-imagined caricature, of Luba. At times I wondered why she alarmed me so, why I was so hard on her, and at that struck-dumb moment, several questions rose in answer: Was it because she was once like me and then fell on her face? Did she remind me that there is still time for me to fall on my face, too?

As the taxi bumped over the old narrow roads, I thought of a Christmas dinner during my first year in college, during which the men in my family played cards around a small square table in the living room, talking about cities and sports, and the women—from my thirteen-year-old cousin to my eighty-three-year-old grandmother—sat at the large oak dinner table, talking about men. The question of what makes an ideal husband floated lightly around the table, and we took turns plucking it from the air.

"Well," began an aunt, "I think it's very important for him to feel comfortable dancing, and to hold the door open for you."

"And he must wear interesting socks!" my mom tossed in.

"And love to watch *The Princess Bride*!" I added.

Several male cousins joined our table. So did my dad. We reversed the question to them: What makes an ideal wife?

One cousin laughed, and in his adolescent cracking voice answered, "First of all, she must never disagree with anything you say. Then. . . ."

His mother whacked him softly on the forehead with a cloth napkin, but then apologized profusely and spent ten minutes tousling his hair. "Someone else, please," she crooned.

We all looked at my dad, who sat tall and relaxed in his chair, listening. One of us asked: "How would you describe an ideal wife?" The corners around his eyes fanned into a semi-sun of wrinkles, and without stirring or speaking he pointed to my mom. At that moment, every single woman at that table from age thirteen to age eighty-three wanted to be looked at, pointed at, loved and chosen and chosen again, the way he had just chosen her. It occurred to me then that while all of the women in my vast extended family had been married not unhappily to their husbands for years, too many of the men still viewed women as girls and their spouses as wives, rather than as the women with whom they had fallen in love. All of the men, that is, except for my dad.

The taxi arrived at the station, and Carl carried our suitcases as we moved through escalators, stairs, hallways. I glanced around distractedly as he asked me for our passports, which I held in my purse, under three folded linen handkerchiefs and a box of camouflage band-aids. "Is everything okay?" he asked.

I nodded, feeling claustrophobic from the crowds and from Carl's worrying. I could not shake the thought of so many men, digging into the most hidden and profound recesses of their being simply to find one perfect hello, one creative date, one topic in common, one moment to calm her, one moment to allow her to calm him, one touch, one kiss, one conversation that could expand forever . . . and finally, one summoning of every hope and courage to ask her (present ring here) for that Forever. Yet somehow, once that Forever is secured, it seemed to me that many women soften and grow needy, while many men harden and retire their digging spades. My mental pie graph began to look like a video-game packman, a yellow circle with a tiny slice towards the center for a mouth. All yellow, a tiny bit of black—my poor chart was yellowing almost all the way around with examples of this post-marriage, or post-confidence-in-something-close-to-marriage phenomenon in which the woman was left empty, and the man, relaxing after his efforts, was not seeing—or not acknowledging—his wife's awareness that she was no longer a recipient of the cordial, attentive smile, the careful listening now turned so easily to all others, to all new men and women, to everyone except herself. And there she is: left vacant, spent, undone, soft.

I was growing annoyed thinking about this, and once, still spinning in the hamster wheel of my thoughts, I flinched when Carl put his arm around my shoulder. "Are you still thinking about this morning?" he asked.

"How could I not be? I don't understand why women stay with men like that. Everything starts off so nicely and then out of nowhere the man turns into *that*—and the woman turns into something worse— I see it everywhere—and she thinks, if this were ten years ago, if she had a job outside the home, if she weren't beaten down by Jasper's rules . . . if she were still young and confident and traveling light, she would leave her husband in a second."

"Who's Jasper?" Carl asked, confused. "Is he in our class in college?"

"Never mind Jasper," I said. "The fact is, you know I'm right. A woman falls in love, her instincts stop working, and she goes soft and dull and unable to speak accurately about anything."

"I don't think that's true," said Carl in a quiet voice as he maneuvered us through a turnstile. I started to argue, but then an even worse thought struck me: What if Carl was right? What if this Luba—this woman who stands for all of our worst nightmares—wouldn't leave? She seems to think her life is perfect.

I waited like a ferocious animal, my eyes sharp, my teeth at the ready, for Carl to speak next. For him to interrupt or point out that I didn't know what sort of relationship the breakfast couple had. To try to calm me by saying something dumb like that love is bind-

ing in more ways than one, and that its facets are all
but invisible to anyone outside. That sometimes people
prick you and you forgive them, and that when you are
truly in love, you don't mind putting up with it.

I knew exactly what he wanted to say, because he
said these things every time I grew flustered after an
argument, claiming that we must not love each other
that much if we still could hurt each other so badly. He
liked to say that sometimes there are parts of love that
we don't understand. Sometimes dysfunctional relationships become happy unions. Love is inexplicable,
he might have said, always a mystery. But I know he
knew that this morning I would have raved back, *How
can that work? How can they stand it?*

And so this morning Carl did not argue.

"You know," he said gently, "I was upset by that, too."

"I will never be that woman."

"Of course you won't!"

We were on the train by this point, but I still wanted
to argue. I was offended, by that man, by all men, and
even by Carl. Recently Carl and I had been arguing
more, much more than we ever did in the months after
we met in class and circled each other hopefully, or during the past year when we had been living near each
other on campus, spending days and nights together in
a sort of practice marriage. I reminded myself that our
arguments were not imbalanced; when we argued we
were equals, we both hurt, we both sometimes said too
much. I did not have reason to fear a future with Carl.
We cared for each other and trusted each other and
made each other laugh, and lately we had been using
"we" when alluding to what lay ahead. Yet this trip,
this thick and borderless time together, had a gaining

permanence that I hadn't felt before, as well as an abrasiveness from seeing each other all the time, not just when we were happy and at our best and excited to be together.

And so I started again: "The thing about Luba . . ."

Carl looked at me exhaustedly and warily, as if I had tipped over some invisible edge. "Who is Luba? That's a weird name. Who are these people you're talking about?"

"They're no one. The thing is that all of these men are colonizing all of these women. Living off their resources—off the *fat* of these women."

Carl, who was studying honors history, knew much more about colonialism than I did. He knew I was making up a metaphor to try to make him feel bad.

And so he responded, "That's true of colonialism in part, but in theory the whole point of colonialism is that the more powerful country is helping the less powerful country to move into the future. They believed it helped them—civilized them. Sure, a lot of it was piracy, like all the treasures we saw in those museums. But sometimes the colonizers did good stuff. They brought the colonies vaccinations, for example . . ."

"After killing them all off with smallpox and syphilis," I interrupted. I didn't know which colonies I was talking about, but it sounded right. "But that's not my point. My point is that marriage takes this precious thing, this woman, *my woman*, and colonizes her into the past—she is a ghost of history, a joke from the 1950s. She becomes just—lost."

"You don't understand," said Carl sadly.

"Neither do you."

But even without Carl's knowledge of world history, I could see that colonizing was what we were all doing—the men who muted their wives; England over how many centuries, lording its power over how many countries; even, I realized, pet stores, and me as their accomplice, in taking hedgehogs from their hedges, inbreeding them, and selling them to people like me, who didn't even know what they ate. And so these once-wild creatures soften their spikes, their feathers and their camouflage and their lean brown bodies, and grow tame, touchable, labile. Finally I was beginning to see why the nightmare of Luba was so hard to wake from.

I was ready to go home. I was baffled by colonialism, tired of thinking about the future with Carl, and sick of wearing unwashed clothes. And I missed Shimmie. She pricked me, peed on my furniture, occasionally bit me, yet I adored her. Whenever she tried to run away from me, long pink legs emerged like a surprise from under her small frame. She had ears like Mickey Mouse, though during the winter they grew chapped and ragged at the edges, making their circles look less compass-drawn and more as if they were magic-markered in a jagged child's hand. Her spikes lurched forward like a crown when she was curious, and when she was angry they parted down the middle like a balding man's comb-over. Her mysteries bewildered me. I loved the softness of her head when she parted her spikes. She would die in a week if I failed to feed her, and yet it was clear she resented my solicitousness. She was dumb, an animal, a rodent—and yet I would starve on a desert island before I would eat her and live.

I looked out the windows of the train at the dry, greenish ground, moving beneath us at many miles an hour, and at the trees and the hedges, the houses and the yards. I wondered which of those homes held inside them couples, married or unmarried; I wondered if the years together had made them apathetic, angry, or habited into joy; I wondered how many of those couples had children; I wondered if any of them were the proud owners of a baby hedgehog.

CARL AND I returned from London after two and a half weeks, stiff and jet-lagged and full of tea, lethargy, and airplane peanuts. We separated after the cab ride back to our neighborhood and I was relieved—and sad at my relief—to be home, back in my own space with my own belongings and with my hedgehog. I left my suitcase in the common room and skidded in my socks across the oak floor, toward Shimmie's covered cage.

But the cover had fallen off—or perhaps my roommate who was feeding her had forgotten to put it on—and Shimmie was nowhere to be found.

I looked around the small space, in the cabinets and behind the bookshelf. I got onto the floor and slinked under furniture on my belly, looking for her. I found nothing. She had completely vanished. I searched in my shoes.

By the time I fell asleep, clothes still on, suitcase still packed, I had given her up for gone. Animals die, I told myself. They run away, they leave us, they disappoint. The loneliness of being the only soul in my dorm room after what felt like a lifetime of sharing tiny spaces with Carl descended. Feeling tragic and defeated, a bereft heroine in a Disney movie, I cried myself to sleep.

A few hours later I woke to a rustling inside the walls, and all of a sudden Shimmie popped out of a half-dollar sized hole in the wall. Like the suspension of physics in giving birth, there was no logical reason why she should have fit. But I was not interested in logic. I did not care where she had been. I was hollow, awash with adoration, astonished at the beauty of her tiny sweet fierce face, and overjoyed to have her back, alive and with me.

I dug my hand underneath her—she pricked me!— and scooped her up and held her to my chest. She had puffs of pink fiberglass caught in her spikes and staticked onto the downy hair of her soft belly. I brushed them off, leaving a cotton-candy trail on the front of my shirt and across my bedroom carpet. She trembled at first, hissed quietly like a teapot, and then relaxed and softened her spikes; she looked up at me with her defiant, beady eyes, and after a moment she licked my thumb, wiped her nose on my palm, and curled into a sleepy ball in my hands.

Toil

1

Girl goes into woods, comes out wiser.

Woods are full of beasts with too many legs. Woods whisper in our dreams. Woods strip us of our logic and tangle our paths; no ladder will stand up against those trees. Woods eat us whole if we dare stay too long. Woods show us for the cowards that we are. Woods take away who we have said we are, and leave us only with who we might be.

The woods are where the action of any story takes place, between the safe arms of the dying mother and the safe castle of the final prince—or in my case, between handsome Gideon the Gilgamesh scholar, waiting for me in Los Angeles; and green-hot-growing Texas, where I would take flight and end up living on my mother's sofa for weeks and weeks until my dad gives me a gentle nudge that it is probably time to find a job and an apartment.

So then, what about the woods?

2

I think this story takes place at night, again and again. It is any long period of time during which women gather, night-music surrounding them, cackling over too much wine. It is any stirred cauldron, any baked pie. This story is not so much a story as a place: the woods.

Was it the present? The past? The future? Was it even September, or had time gone flat? Was it a circle of hell or heaven, a moebius strip of endless hot minutes: glowing, right on the edge of turning to ash? Did the night last as long as it took to prepare, bake, eat, and clean up a pie? Am I still there, one foot caught forever in that night, at Porcia's half-built house in the woods?

I think I was twenty-four. I know I had been in love. I know that the women who had taught me to write were dying, all of them turning into ash and dying, and soon I would be the only one left among us, carrier of our collective stories. Our teacher's life was hanging from a thread, but this was as it should be—hadn't I made her a toast at her hundredth birthday just a year ago? Hadn't she said she didn't want to live to the next election out of fear for what her country might become?

Still, I left my dog and my apartment and my boyfriend and my graduate fellowship and every other thing I had worked to keep alive. I flew across the country, from the warmth of endless-summer California to the moody, darkening autumn of New England. I thought that, in the end, none of it mattered except the writing, and here was the woman who taught me to write, and I needed to see her to the end.

My life as I knew it was about to fall apart. Did I not know? I think I must've known. But I couldn't have known how much. Was this what is called a quarter-life crisis? I left my life in a fragile, still beating state to make a final visit to Hope Hale Davis, dying author, ex-communist, four times widow, the crone in my first fairy tale, the good Baba Yaga who said, *Toil, toil, and if you ever stop toiling, the world and I will eat you up.*

3

The day I spent in the hospital, but I had nowhere to stay the night. "Take the bus to Vermont," my friend Hattie said. "We'll pick you up." On the bus I sat next to a man who commented on my sad face and told me about his life, and after an hour he asked if I'd take the train with him from here to San Francisco. No, I said. He said he'd wait for me at the station tomorrow in case I changed my mind.

Hattie was waiting at the bus stop and we hugged and hugged in the car, for it had been over a year. We stopped at a fruit stand to buy apples and a *New York Times*. For Porcia, she said, who owned the house where we would stay.

The man selling fruit looked about a hundred years old. As old as Hope. Hattie teased him a little and he teased her back. "Goodbye, God!" she said in her joyful birdsong voice, and then to me she said, "I always tell him that I think he looks like God. Or the way you'd imagine God looking."

I remember how lovely and healthy my friend looked. Her hair had grown long and she had stopped bleaching it. She was smiling, looking fresh-scrubbed; muscle had replaced the softness of her arms. But she was otherwise just the same. She always had a slow-motion feel to the way she lived and talked. She attributed it to having grown up in the leisurely South, but it was more than that. Once she fell backwards in a chair in a coffee shop while we were cramming last-minute for our world religions exam, and she managed to fall while holding her full mug at a balance so as not to spill one single drop. She was always doing these magical things, with apparent ease, and laughing amazedly at herself as she did so.

We drove through trees and trees, down a dirt driveway that must've been half a mile long, before we came to a timber house with a long-haired woman outside, gathering moss. "Come meet Porcia," Hattie said, with a slightly higher uptick in her voice.

Porcia was leaning over the ground, gathering moss into a basket. She had gray streaks in her hair and a face that looked angry when resting; she wore patchy clothes. Two wolfish dogs flanked her, and gave a mild *woof.* She waved but did not engage.

Hattie told me while we unpacked that Porcia was a professor at the Divinity School, but then she got divorced and had a falling out with someone in the department and moved to Vermont where her parents had a house.

Here's how I remember her house:

Unfinished.

It was something her father left and she was living in, and when I was there she was gathering the skills, slowly, slowly, to complete the work. In my memory, it was a one-room cabin with an upstairs loft, and we spent forever and a day in the kitchen and living room, sitting across three hard chairs, and sometimes moving across the room to sit on the old sofa and the rug. It felt somehow that the whole house was a library, for in addition to the usual shelves, rising in the room's center was an unfinished staircase of planky unpolished wood with books packed like insulation underneath each step. Books filled every permeable space in this room; they formed side-tables, ledges beneath windows; they were scattered around the floor, lined up against the unfinished walls, and in the kitchen, wedged next to mugs and plates. Amid all the books, a few framed Arthur Rackham prints leaned against walls, unhung: Miss Muffett, Three Little Pigs, and Woman being clasped by a Tree-Man. Red Riding Hood.

4

We unloaded apples and I learned that there was no indoor bathroom and that I'd sleep with Hattie in a smaller cabin a quarter mile further into the woods. That in this house, Porcia slept alone.

Hattie wanted to know all about Hope. I told Hattie how she lost her false teeth in the popcorn I brought her. How all day she flirted with the male nurses. Then I heard a sudden sound, a bark of a laugh at this innocence. It was Porcia.

I told them both, "She's dying. I'll spend tomorrow with her, and then I fly back to LA."

"Why?" Porcia asked. It was the first time I'd heard her voice. It had a demanding, eroded quality, as if it were made of sand and rock and midden and earth.

I told her that it was where my life awaited: my dog, my PhD program, my boyfriend, my overpriced roachy apartment in front of which I always got parking tickets, because this was LA.

"So you've just come out to watch your mentor fall." She turned to Hattie. "You watched me fall."

Hattie nodded almost imperceptibly. Porcia picked up the apples. "You showed grace when I did." She looked straight at me.

"The mentor always falls," Hattie said agreeably. "Just when the girl is most lost in the woods. I remember when Porcia told me that. I'm sorry, honey," she said to me, "about Hope."

Porcia began to chop apples. We watched her add spices and suddenly it was like a spell was cast and the whole house smelled of cardamom and cinnamon. She turned a crust, pinching it. She worked quietly and I realized Hattie and I had stopped our talking to watch Porcia's hands. Porcia had a capacity for silence that I had never seen before or since. It was monastic, hinting at endless root structures; it was not clear if it held a monk's peace.

Porcia put the pie in the oven and wiped her hands on her jeans. Then Hattie asked me, "How early do you need to leave?"

"I'll need to take the earliest bus."

Porcia said, "That means waking up at four."

"Should we sleep?" I asked.

"You should always sleep."

"It's true," Hattie agreed. "That way you can live as long as God at the apple stand."

"Longer," said Porcia. "Women last longer."

Porcia left jagged and ominous silences at the ends of her pronouncements, which Hattie filled with questions, for which I was grateful.

"So do you like grad school? No, wait. First tell me about Gideon. He's really handsome!"

And we went from there. Our shared future in libraries. Our plans after LA. His Gilgamesh. How he's younger than me by two years. Shy, smart. Wants to get married.

Porcia watched me for a long time. "So you think he's safe," she said at last.

5

"Safety in men is a good thing," Hattie said, as if she had been musing on it a long time, rather than just laying floorboards beneath our conversation so that Porcia and I would not fall through. "I followed a restless wandering type—you know, a poet—across France. I could learn a thing or two from you. Does Gideon want to be a writer, like you?"

"No. He wants to study writing, because in his words who—besides Hope and people born in 1900—can make a living writing? I'll wake up early and write in the morning, before I have to go do other things."

"You could write all day if you lived out here," Porcia said without looking at either of us.

Hattie burst out in generous laughter. "But then you'd have to live out here."

"I prefer cities," I said, not looking at Porcia.

"Even though it means fighting with other rats to make enough money to pay for your leaky cold apartment to get hot water and heat?"

I thought of LA, where I shared an apartment entry with a masseuse named Lone Wolf who had two dogs, both half-wolf, who threw themselves against his front door whenever anyone walked down our hall. His wolves wanted to eat my dog. Their fleas spread across the old red carpet, to my dog, to me. In LA, the roaches waited behind the appliances, behind the taps with their spill of yellow water, coming out in the darkness. When you turned on the lights suddenly to get water at night, they all scattered. Outside in our garden, our collective trash festered. My dog liked to stop and smell it on our walks.

Hattie said buoyantly, as if reading my mind: "You might live somewhere better than that."

Porcia stroked her dog's haunches. "I loathe how dependent cities make people."

"I suppose you can't depend on anyone out here," I said with care, hoping not to get into an argument with Porcia. "But you lived in cities before. For how long?"

"For as long as I was willing to sell my soul, first to my husband, then to the Dean."

Hattie said, "Porcia wrote this amazing book the year she finished law school. She did law school and a PhD at the same time."

"Jesus. Who does that?"

Porcia looked up from the animal, long crimped hairs falling from her hands. "People like me. Like you."

Hattie kept talking. I knew this was her way of getting out of trouble, one she had learned in the South from her mother, because my mother in a different part of the South had taught me the same thing. When in doubt, just keep talking and talking and talking.

"Her book was about labor as religious meditation. She looked at monasteries from 1400 up until today. It was an amazing book. I read excerpts of it in a class, and that's why I wanted to learn from Porcia."

"Do you write anymore?" I asked.

"No. I'm retired. Like your writing teacher."

"She's not retired. She was still teaching two weeks ago, until she fell. She was still writing, too. The last time I saw her before she went into hospice, she asked me to help her edit a story from her files. She wrote stories for *The New Yorker* when it was a young magazine and her goal is to get published there just one more time before she dies."

"That's terrible."

"I don't think it's terrible."

"It's pathetic."

"I think it's hopeful," said Hattie.

"So do I," I said.

Porcia stood. "You two start on dinner. I'm going upstairs to nap."

"Should I bring you up some tea?" Hattie asked.

"Don't act as if I'm a little old lady."

I thought, as Porcia and her dogs ascended, of a line I read in one of my grad school books: *frequent napping is suicide in women.*

6

I wasn't sure what to say around Porcia, and I felt relieved when she vanished into the darkness above the splintery stairs; but she came down soon enough. Hattie opened the wine and marinated the lamb and retrieved a box of hats that she said we might wear for dinner. She took out a pink baseball cap with a tattered pair of pink felt boobs ballooning on its top and placed it on her head.

After one glass of wine, Porcia began to talk. I learned that she fell hard for one of her students her final summer of teaching. He was twenty-one. She was forty-eight. She told him that she thought he was the most beautiful person she had ever met and that he gave her hope that people were okay after all. She was planning already to move to the woods, to retire or to hibernate or to just wait out a season. Her student had wanted to move out here with her, but she was still married and he had a life to live. When she broke up with him so she wouldn't cripple his future, he had said, "I can't believe the author of that book is just going to live out there like a witch. You have too much to offer the world." Then you go and offer it, Porcia had told him.

"Both my degrees were a means to an end, and it turned out to be the wrong end. I went into academia because I had questions about humans and solitude and work. I went into law because I thought it would make me stand out as an academic. My former husband thought it was all great. He liked the work. To me it was meaningless. I should've avoided school and done work with my hands instead. All you do with any learning is the same. Join the forces."

Porcia raised her arms to push back her sleeves, and the smell of ripe body odor filled the small area. Hattie noticed and wrinkled her nose, and Porcia looked at her as if to say, *stop caring.*

"So let me tell you ze story of ze man who was my amour in Pareez," Hattie said, in charmingly botched English-French. "I followed him to Paris because I thought if he was ever going to realize that he couldn't resist me, it would be there."

"It didn't work?"

"No," Porcia said. "She lasted about a month and a half, nobody would hire her and the boy thought she was a messy roommate, and so they broke up. But still you waited around for a few more weeks." Porcia was looking hard at Hattie. "You should never have gone."

"Oh, I don't know."

When I needed a bathroom Porcia tossed me a roll of toilet paper and pointed outside. I walked a dusky half-mile to the end of the driveway, where I called Gideon and got no answer but was able to listen to a message he had left me. It was angry. Angry for leaving school to come here. Angry for being away on a futile goodbye mission. Angry for not prioritizing future over past.

Is it all, then, for my remembering self? Myself at Hope's age? All of the life between here and there: Do you do it to remember having done it? It seems so many things are this way, while the experiencing self simply wants to rest, to lie in the moss, to call it a day.

7

"Hey!" Hattie cried, jumping up. "Do you want to know how to fit a bra properly?" She dragged into the room a small chest containing clothes and many bras.

I picked them up one by one, a gorgeous swell of petals in every color. It was the most color in the room, in the house, in the woods. That night, it felt like the most color I had seen in my life.

"They're from Fig Leaf—the lingerie store where I work part-time." She handed me a red bra with delicate daisy lacing and then said: "I wonder when I'll be too old to be a ne'er-do-well."

"Maybe never," offered Porcia. She had shed her grave, vacant, window-staring look and was narrowing her eyes at us again.

Hattie said thoughtfully, "One day I'll grow."

"Growth is overrated," Porcia said shortly, while I turned my back and put on the bra.

"Okay." Hattie leaned over me, her hands warm and capable, giving instructions. "Lean forward so that your breasts fit into the cups using gravity. Then adjust the straps so that it comes low on your back. Much lower than that. You want it beneath your shoulder blades. That gives the right support. Now for the clasps. Start on the outside one. Does that feel like it fits?"

"It's looser than I usually do it."

"That's okay. All fabrics get elastic as they age, so you want to start with the widest band and move in as you need it. There. Fits perfectly." She laughed as she looked at me. "This is the culmination of my professional skill."

Then Hattie unhooked the bra and jumped up again and cried, "You should pick your hats!" She opened the box and held out an armful. "We wear hats to dinner. You've got to mark the day somehow or else you'll lose your mind."

"I think your mind is only susceptible to loss," Porcia said to Hattie, "because you don't know what you want your life to be. My mind isn't. Not anymore. If you wanted, you could make a new life work."

We were all silent again.

Hattie said nothing, so I thought I'd build our next floor. I picked up a cowboy hat with leather straps and handed it to Porcia. "How's this one?"

She handed me a wide-brimmed hat glowing with yellow daisies.

"My favorite is the boob hat," said Hattie. "The one Porcia's ex-husband won at a carnival."

"I bet he sorely misses it," I said, feeling a little looser around her.

She stared at me long. "Yes."

Now Hattie was trying the red bra on the boob hat. She pulled the bra around to the front so that the hat tipped off and fell. Porcia picked it up and set it on the side of the table.

Hattie sipped her wine thoughtfully. "I don't know why this career thing has been such a problem. Sometimes I think I'm brilliant because I see that jobs don't really matter, and other times I'm pretty sure I'm just lazy. I really don't know what the hell I'm doing."

"Just get a PhD. It'll be easy. You can do it in a few years. If you hate it you can go do something else, or stop midway through."

"You are so damned innocent," Porcia said, but her voice was gentler than usual. "Committed to your gardens. To your ladders. Your cities."

Did I have an answer for her? Wine made it easier not to speak. I read in one of my graduate school books that schizophrenic patients are often left in gardens to read and paint, because gardens are so safe. But I wonder if that's such a good idea. I mean, dangerous things can get into gardens, just like any safe space. Isn't that the point? That we long for the solace of enclosed gardens because of some old broken Adam-and-Eve notion? It seemed that important things happened in gardens. Depending on the story, they happened in gardens or in the woods.

"I don't want to live in the South," Hattie said, intruding into my thought-garden with a hiccup. "I don't want to work for an asshole."

8

We were leaning around in the kitchen, surrounded by books, waiting for the meat to grill, as well as some vegetables dug from the garden. Porcia kept speaking to the window more than to us; once she said, "I like it because it smells like the beginning of the world here— before the world fell."

Porcia, it seemed, thought a lot about falls. I wonder if she could see I was about to have one. All of the losses were coming at once. I could feel their closeness, their tapping at the garden wall. I cannot remember a word of what I said as we waited for dinner to be ready, except that it was all about safety, certainty, harried attempts to pull my gardens into me, closer and closer. Gideon. LA. The PhD.

"Once upon a time I felt certain of things," said Porcia, as we waited. "I believed in gardens."

She told us that her former husband, an ex-theologian, had wanted to understand nature and how it relates to God.

"Hey!" said Hattie. "That's what I'm trying to understand!"

"I know," said Porcia, quieting her. "We both were worried about what the hell to do with God."

In the end, the husband hung himself.

"In this house?" Hattie asked in a whisper. "I thought you just got divorced."

Porcia did not answer, which I took to mean yes. Hattie and I met eyes for the briefest of looks. I wondered if she was feeling what I was feeling, which was a childish sense of relief at not having to sleep in the house. I wondered how Porcia did it, this living with a ghost—one of many ghosts, it appeared. Of course, Porcia saw our look, and it seemed, for an asymptotic flicker of a moment, that she was smiling at us.

"This is a good place to be a widow," she said at last. "A good place to toil."

I thought of something I had read in the Bible the one time I attempted to read it—in the world religions class where Hattie and I barely passed the exam, but she made the miracle-save of tipping over backwards without spilling her coffee while studying. My thought was how Adam had to work for his food after the expulsion but not before. Toil, it seemed, was a punishment. Yet I felt short-breathed and void-scared at the thought of life without it.

Now Hattie was asking questions about Porcia's marriage, and Porcia was fending them off, saying, "I remember being your age, when these things mattered."

"How could they not matter?" Hattie insisted.

"Because they happen to everyone. Go read any story. People were in love. Then they weren't. Then somebody died. They're not my stories."

"But this story happened to *you*."

Porcia reflected for a moment. Then she opened her mouth, closed it, and opened it again. "There was a child," she said at last.

"WHAAAT?!" Hattie swiveled in her chair so fast that the boob-hat tumbled off. She put it back on and stared at Porcia.

"Not a living one."

"What?" Hattie tried again in a whisper.

"I had a stillborn. Do you know about those? Was that part of your education?" She looked away from us. "We had a stillborn baby and got to watch it being thrown away. And after that my husband decided he wanted to inseminate some younger women who could have living babies. I let him go—that part was easy. Then he came back after a year, right after my father died, and said he was wrong, it wasn't about the baby. He wanted to try again. But that wasn't what he wanted. He wanted a quiet place to die in the woods. And he got that."

"The moss sculptures that you and I make and sell? They are from the moss that grows over their graves. The ashes of the baby—I wouldn't let the midwife tell me if it was a boy or a girl. And its father."

9

"Should we check on the meat?" Hattie asked, jumping up and pouring syrupy noise into the silence after Porcia's story. Porcia went outside and we heard the sudden sound of dogs howling from the darkness outside the open door.

"Why are they barking?" I asked nervously.

"Impossible to know. We have a lot of sounds here. It frightened me, too, at first."

"What if it's a burglar?" I said.

Hattie shrugged, tipsy and unconcerned. "It could be a ghost."

A knock on the door, and we both jumped. The dogs were still going crazy outside. Hattie opened the door—my temptation was to bar it—and it was Porcia, hands full with the grilled meat on a plate. In silence, we filled plates and began eating.

We were all three wearing absurd hats. Porcia had settled on a sergeant's metal helmet; I had a straw basket hat with plastic fruit on top, while Hattie still wore the boob-hat.

"So there's no phone here," I said after a while. "What about internet?"

Hattie chewed and swallowed. "You have to go into town."

"So—what if there's an emergency?" I said, taking a deep breath.

"What kind of emergency could happen out here?" Porcia demanded. "You worry a lot."

"Suppose you choke on something."

"Wouldn't happen. I chew my food carefully."

"Do you know first aid?"

"I know enough. What's the worst that can happen?"

"Die."

Porcia reflected and dismissed this idea. "People have been doing this for years. You survive on what you have, and if something goes wrong you either deal with it or die. It doesn't worry me. But if you need to make a phone call, the next-door neighbor is a mile east—Hattie can show you."

"No. I don't want to go outside at night. It creeps me out that nobody can reach us out here."

"Here, we are blessedly unreachable. It's the only way to learn to trust yourself."

Finally, the dogs quieted. In the wake of their silence, Hattie said, "Trust yourself. That's what I wish my mother had told me. You should be a life coach, Porcia. You're as wise as a mother."

"Well, I'm not either and I never will be."

Porcia scratched her eyebrow with a long fingernail.

"The only time I ever had trouble out here was with a man who delivered firewood and then kept coming back at night. I kept finding him looking in the windows while I was cooking dinner. Each time I sent Bo outside, and that usually got him to leave. Bo's a good watch dog. After a few months I got tired of it and called the police. They wanted to know what he had done, and he hadn't done anything—he was just creepy. One officer came to look around, and finally he told me, 'Look sweetheart, if you intend to live out here all alone, you can't call us every time a person looks creepy.'"

She went on: "The weirdest visitor I had was a spider. It came about a month after my dad died. The day I was getting rid of books. On one of the shelves I saw the biggest spider I had ever seen. It was sitting on top of Marcus Aurelius." She held out her hand, thumb and middle finger about three inches apart. "It wasn't a tarantula or a daddy-long legs—it looked like an ordinary wolf spider, but it was enormous."

"How big are black widows?" I asked.

"Small. This was much bigger than that. I'm not superstitious and I don't believe in anthropomorphizing things, but I know this spider was watching me. Eventually I went upstairs to bed and the next day it was still there—in the kitchen, on the dining table. I tried to lead it onto a piece of paper and drop it outside, but it crawled off the paper onto the floor and stayed. It kept appearing around the house for the rest of the week. I didn't want to kill it."

Porcia studied our faces closely. "I didn't want to kill it because I think it was my dad."

Hattie and I sat silent. There was nothing to say.

"So finally, when I found it in my bathroom when I was getting ready for bed, I talked to it. I said, 'Hi Dad. You've seen that I'm all right. You don't have to look after me. You can go now.' And, that moment, the spider walked off of the counter and across the floor toward the window, and I never saw him again."

10

I used to have a theory that women spend their lives weaving webs for widowhood. Porcia seemed to be both the proof and the exception. She was spending her widowhood avoiding using her life. I was afraid to believe the things she believed.

As we cleaned up, Hattie leaned back against a kitchen wall and a tower of books toppled over on her. "How are you, honey?" she asked, as we put the books away. "You look like you're tired."

I was, and I told her so.

"They've captured you, honey. You work too hard. You need to return to a handmade life. Stay."

I thought, *I can't.* If I stayed even another night I would never restart. The LA life was the wrong life, my toil on that coast was the wrong toil. But to stop now, to stay in these mossy woods any longer . . .

Porcia said from the sofa, "Come sit, both of you. Think of a question you have about your life now. Think hard." We sat.

I knew my question without having to think. It was about work versus leisure, toil versus retirement, Hope versus Porcia, Gideon versus Porcia's buried husband. The truth is that it felt I had been doing only work for years. Even my relationship felt like labor to secure something that I wasn't sure I wanted. The working to afford a house, to maintain a house, to earn the necessary credentials, not to waste my education, to keep working all my life . . .

Porcia handed us a small leather bag, into which we both dug and each pulled out a small flat stone, the size of a scrabble piece. "Show me what you have."

"I have Man again," said Hattie. She took the boob-hat off her head solemnly.

"I knew you would." To me, Porcia said: "*Mannaz* means human. Hattie will leave here soon and return to the world of them."

Mine was just a straight line. I handed it to Porcia, who examined it, put it back into the bag, and read from a small book on the table: "*Isa*, Ice. Rune of stasis and the ego-self. *Isa* represents immobility, a halt in activity until a change takes place, the way icicles form in winter and must wait until spring to turn back into the fluid state and become free." She repeated, looking at me straight: "Turn back into the fluid state and become free."

Then Porcia dug in the bag and picked one for herself. "*Othala*," she said. "Home. This rune represents home of a sacred ancestral nature. It represents wealth, but a wealth that cannot be sold, only passed down or inherited. *Othala* represents enclosure. Look for tall walls protecting the existing state of things, where wealth continues flourishing inside."

Porcia went quiet, thinking. At last she said, "I think we are three Eves, all equally expelled."

We reflected on this, then another bottle of wine materialized and Hattie and Porcia spent an hour heckling each other about their futures.

"I've done everything I set out to do," Porcia said. "I'm done. But you—you haven't even begun."

"I know," Hattie said in a mournful voice. "When I leave here I am going to do something. Maybe I'll apply to medical school."

"You should join New Beginnings Anonymous."

"Is there such an organization? If not—hey! Maybe that's what I'll start!"

"Just figure out what you want to give yourself to, Hattie."

"So far, I've given my life mostly to useless men," she said, her hands cupping the boob-hat still on her lap.

"I gave mine to knowledge," Porcia said bitterly. "Now to moss sculptures and living out here like a hermit."

Then they both looked at me.

11

I think, as I peer back into this night in the woods, of an essay I read in *The American Scholar* by William Dere- siewicz, who asks the question: "What happens when busyness and sociability leave no room for solitude? The ability to engage in introspection [is] the essen- tial precondition for living an intellectual life, and the essential precondition for introspection is solitude."

Porcia was the first woman I knew who had such a capacity for solitude; Hope was the first woman I knew who lived to a hundred, outliving everyone she loved: a writer, teacher, mother, just as I hoped to one day be. Hope outlived four husbands, had three children, kept writing and teaching until she died, lived in the thick of the world. Porcia outlived one husband and retired to the cabin to opt out of whatever miles to go remained before she could sleep.

I wanted to contribute. I wanted children (though not, I knew, with Gideon). I was attracted to the life of the woods but didn't want to stay in seclusion forever. Yet it felt tempting.

Back then, I never would've imagined my capacity for solitude, though my life today is marked by it. Like Porcia. Like Hope.

Porcia seemed unknowable: she could do anything and it would not come as a shock. She could live in the woods forever with a spider and dogs for company. Or she could change her mind, return to the knowledge universe, and burn the place down.

Both she and Hope had lived all the stories I both longed for and dreaded—and survived each one so differently. In the city, striving. In the woods, mossed over. It is a spidery weaving, this being a woman. It means wondering what it would have looked like, if it had not been this life. It means asking hard questions of the days in front of me, spindly long-legged questions that sometimes feel like they'd be better off hiding under tables and chairs.

It is rare that I dream about the woods, but when I do it takes me out for several days. Those days I reconsider. I do not work well. I drink only tea and forget about water.

Could it be that we all have those days? Perhaps some people do not look back in this same way, do not waste time in straining backward, wondering—

While my life is marked by its almosts.

I picture Porcia in the cabin still—alone, or with her father the spider. She is making a pie crust. How does a woman become so wounded? How can a university devour its young in such a way? Do such wounds ever heal? There she is still, half-way between my age now, forty, and Hope's age when I met her. I watch her assess her spices and mix them with ancient kitchen instruments. Sometimes a strange man prowls the trees around her cabin; the police do or do not come when she calls. Sometimes a spider visits her, though never the same one. Dogs bark, birds cry. Porcia starts, then goes back to her work.

12

At the night's end, we ate Porcia's numinous pie and drank more wine and shouted out "Double, double, toil and trouble; fire burn and cauldron bubble" to the windless, crickety night. Hattie got gloriously drunk and crashed around the house singing, "Crisp bacon is the love of the me! I wish I were a big piece of bacon so I could nibble on my arms!" and "Why did they dress me in my pajamas?" Then she yelped, "I want to have sex!" for about half an hour, and tried to think of men she might call, but was thwarted obviously by the lack of cell phone reception. "I will eat of the plant!" Hattie screeched, and clamped down like an alligator on Porcia's houseplant.

Porcia stood at the base of the stairs as if she wanted to offer some last word on the night, but I was too earnest and Hattie was too drunk, so instead she glared and went up to bed, looking as if she might burn the house down with us in it. *Twenty-somethings*, you could almost hear her thinking.

It was really a night of listening, I thought on the plane the next evening, after the long winding bus ride in the frigid New England dawn, after the day holding Hope's frail hand. Listening to someone like me, to someone not-me. To two women who had never known Hope and who never would meet Gideon, but who witnessed my mourning of both.

I love you and I will eat you up, says Baba Yaga in the woods, *so the world doesn't eat you up first.*

Here is your paper and your pen. Have you stopped toiling? Do not you dare! I dream on the bus and in the air of Hope, who in twenty-four hours would take her last breath.

Back in LA, I grasped the dog and gave my futon to my neighbor and moved back to Texas in a dizzy week and fell into my mother's arms. I was damned, damned, dizzy and damned.

But I was not falling apart, I was just growing trees. It would be decades before any of us knew. My trees, my woods, my felled logs and soil covering all of my loves, fears, and almosts—all of that would outlive the dog, the former boyfriend's career as a Gilgamesh scholar, and everything else I cared about in my twenties. Rock bottom wasn't rock bottom, it was just moss. I could land softly, I would wait out my opportunities, I could live under a table like a spider; there would be another way. Those woods would give way to another way to live.

13

Girl goes into the woods and likes the woods. She becomes one of the creatures who live there: stirring, cackling, toiling and troubling. Sometimes she is afraid of herself, but she doesn't have to be. She says to the whole world, *I love you and I love you. I will keep eating you up.*

The Scream

IN JAPANESE, the word *makeru* means to fuck up. It's not a nice word. Its past tense is *maketa*. Which sounds a lot like my last name. So in Japanese, *maketa* means I fucked up. I lose. When the McKetta family rolled off the airplane from Texas to Osaka, Japan, we were a bad system from the get-go.

We were in Japan to visit my sixteen-year-old brother, John, who was spending his sophomore year of high school in Osaka, living with a host family. John had adapted very well—he was mostly fluent, even down to having a Japanese sense of humor, and he also had a twenty-three-year-old Japanese girlfriend. He took us from the airport to a popular restaurant to eat dinner.

And there we all were. My mother, who makes friends with anyone, was smiling and gesturing wildly at the server and asking him getting-to-know-you questions in VERY . . . SLOW . . . ENGLISH. The server was looking at her curiously. My sister Sarah was sitting across from me. She had pulled every bowl of rice over to her spot at the table and was eating it all. She was and is still a vegan—the most cheerful, buoyant, flexible vegan you've ever met—and she'd done her research and learned that there would be fish flakes in everything. So everywhere we went, she bulked up on rice, like a sumo wrestler. She was the only one of us who gained weight throughout the trip. Dishes of food kept arriving, and I asked John to ask the server what it was exactly that we were eating. The server answered and John translated back. "The elbows!"

John was pulling at his hair, something he does when he gets stressed or embarrassed. He apologized to the server for our chaos. When I asked him to translate, he said that he had said "I'm sorry," but the form of I'm sorry that is appropriate for apologizing to strangers for something you did not actually do. It turns out there are over twenty different ways to say I'm sorry in Japanese.

A dish arrived at our table that made the waiters and my brother excited. It was *fugu*, the famous blowfish that is poisonous if you eat the wrong part but for some reason is a coveted dish that travelers, including us, can't leave the country without trying, and you have to trust that your chef knows how to cut it just right, otherwise you'll die. That night I ate it because I wanted to be a good traveler—and then I spent all night awake thinking how the fish didn't even taste very good and I probably was going to die.

Our second day in Japan we took the subway to a marketplace where we were supposed to see an important monument. John led us to the subway, which he rode every day to get to school. On the subway platform there were white-gloved employees who pushed and pushed and squished everyone onto the cars, using their hands, packing people on as tightly as they would fit.

No reasonable animal would enter into this subway car. A dog would bolt. Only tamed, idiotic humans would walk on in. My body knew this. But my mind said, *Shut up, just get on the subway.*

So I got on.

And on the subway, nobody could move and nobody made eye contact. But people did occasionally grab each other, and only later did I learn that there's a phrase in Japanese, *"Koh reh wah dare no te deska!"* that you're supposed to yell out when somebody gropes you on the subway. It translates roughly to "Whose hand is this?" I told myself to stay calm until we got to the market. The market was very nearly as crowded as the subway; you couldn't move without people touching you. Even then, somehow, I managed to get lost, which happens to me a lot, but generally I don't mind because I can ask for directions. But here I panicked because who could I ask? We didn't have phones. I didn't speak the language. By the time my family found me, I was spooked and shaky and felt like a glitchy, problematic four-year-old.

We finally made it to the important monument, but we couldn't see it because between us and the monument were about ten thousand people holding up their camera-phones to take a photo of the monument. All I could see were ten thousand photos.

TEN DAYS into the trip we ate a special New Year's Eve luncheon with John's host family, who were all extremely kind and patient. We took off our shoes and sat at a table where our feet dangled over this space

heater and they served more animal dishes I didn't recognize, as well as a gooey rice soup that reminded me
of silly-putty. My mom was making friends with the
host mother. Sarah had all the bowls of rice in front
of her. John was making jokes in Japanese. The host
father kindly asked, "How is your visit?" Mom and
Sarah both gushed over the monuments and the mar-
kets and the food. They looked at me and I went mute.
I couldn't speak. There was nothing true I felt I could
say. Everything felt so crowded and loud and confus-
ing and unreasonable. And I also felt this incredible
self-loathing. Here I was, with this great opportunity
to be in a country I had never visited, which I probably
wouldn't have the chance to visit again, and I was having a perfectly horrible time. I was a glitch in the system. I couldn't appreciate the travel. I just wanted to
go home, back to my quiet basement apartment where
I lived with my dog and my books and my ordinary
American foods.

I didn't say anything. I couldn't. John said something quietly to his host parents that I'm sure was one
of the twenty-plus versions of "I'm sorry."

We had return tickets for January fifth. Later that
afternoon, on New Year's Eve, I asked Mom and Sarah
how they'd feel if we changed our tickets up a few days
to go home early. They agreed that that was a good
idea; though they were infinitely better travelers than
I, they were also ready.

We called the Japanese airline from our hotel in
Osaka and told them that we would like to leave early.
And they said that all the flights were crowded, because
it was around the new year, and our flight home on the
fifth was a full flight, but we could go standby if we

wanted on a flight on the second, which was two days from then. And we said, "Yes, that's great, yes, thank you, thank you, thank you," and hung up the phone, and then my sister Sarah said, "Wait—did we just agree to give up our tickets home in order to take a standby flight?" and we all said to each other, "No, no, no, that couldn't—no, no, no, surely the system must be better than that, surely they wouldn't've canceled our tickets."

But we called back just to be sure. And this time we were put through a whole rigmarole of systems to find someone who could speak English and tell us, "In fact, no, you don't have a ticket home. You gave up your ticket and since then that flight has filled. We're sorry. Perhaps you can come into our Japan Air office tomorrow and we can see what we can do."

We packed up the following morning, left Osaka, and got on the train to Tokyo. In the station, we had fun looking at the vending machines that sold everything from the normal plastic-wrapped snack foods to gourmet hot drinks to underwear, and then we walked to Japan Air.

It was a very quiet office. It was by far the quietest, most peaceful place we had visited in Japan. There were no lines, they were getting through people very quickly, people were sitting down—everyone was talking in quiet, well-mannered voices. It felt like a place where life ran smoothly in a gentle, predictable whirl.

We were beckoned to a desk where we explained our predicament. The woman at the desk said, "Oh, I see. Well—" her English was excellent—"well, you don't have a flight home. It's unlikely that you'll get on that standby flight because it's full and you're at the end of the standby list. But—there are three seats, not together, but three seats available on a flight leaving Tokyo on January twentieth. Is that going to be okay?"

We had arrived in Japan on December twentieth, spent Christmas there, had tickets to go home on the fifth, had tried to move them to the second, and now were being told we couldn't go home until January twentieth.

"Is that okay?" she asked. "That's all I have."

She looked guilty, and it was obvious she knew we weren't happy, but what could she do, what could we do, what could anybody do? It was a bad system. Air travel is a bad system. And moving your flight is a bad system, and in Japan, McKettas were a bad system.

She started filling out our names to book us on the flight on January twentieth, but before she did she looked up and met my mother's eyes. She said, "I'm sorry."

Then she asked, "Is this going to be okay?"

She looked first at my mom, and my mom, not wanting to be a difficult traveler and seeing no real choice, nodded. And she looked at my sister, who, after a minute, nodded too, because what was she going to do? And then at my brother, who was going to stay in Japan anyway, but was now stuck with us for nearly an extra month, and he also nodded. Then the woman from Japan Air looked at me. "Will this be okay?"

I had so many feelings that I couldn't say, I didn't even know where to start. I didn't have the words to articulate them in English, let alone any words that would translate. Everything felt so completely unreasonable, from eating the elbow and the poisoned fish to having to ask "whose hand is this?" on the subway . . .

and everyone else, everyone at Japan Air, everyone in my family, just went along, acting as if it were all perfectly reasonable. And now here we were, being told that we had to stay for three more weeks. I felt helpless: a twenty-four-year-old trapped on a vacation that just wouldn't end. And the fact that nobody else seemed to mind made me feel like a crazy person. I could tell that they were all waiting for me to speak and I opened my mouth to respond and what came out was . . .

INSERT LOUDEST EVER IMAGINABLE SCREAM HERE

Never before, and never since, has a noise come out of my body like that. Not during a nightmare; not during childbirth; not cheering on my team in a sport match. It was a magnificent scream, a scream at the highest pitch I could have imagined, a scream that took nearly ten seconds to fully emerge. I learned later that my scream leveled the room. It caused everybody to look up, petrified at what would cause a human to make such a sound.

But at the time, my mind was empty: the scream had hollowed it all out.

Then I ran outside and started crying. My brother and sister followed me. John was acutely concerned and kept asking, "Sister, are you okay?" He kept holding my hand and he later said it was out of fear that I'd run off across Tokyo and never be seen again. Sarah thought it was hilarious and couldn't stop laughing. We waited outside for my mom, because I didn't want to go back in there again.

Sarah was ecstatic at what had happened. "I only have three complete stories," she explained. "One is the hot air balloon crash, I can't remember what the second one is, and now I've got Liz screaming in Japan Air."

Sarah loved it; John, I think, thought I had cracked, but was trying to be kind about it. What both of them were too kind to say was that I had made an unforgiveable cultural error. I had *maketa*-ed.

I felt in the aftermath of the scream a rising balloon-like feeling of ecstasy. Release, relief, and a bizarre sense of survivor's joy, though I still didn't know how we were going to get home. There aren't a lot of moments when we lose ourselves entirely. It is terrifying—and also thrilling—to go to the edge and come back. Maybe the problem wasn't just me. Maybe our trip there actually was a bad system, one unreasonable moment after another, and I was the only one willing to scream about it. Words don't usually fail me. But there, the whole trip had disoriented me, pushed me away from my recognizable sane human self to something else, something primal. When I told my four-year-old daughter this story over a decade later, she nodded very understandingly and asked, "Did your mother not bring any of your toys?"

When I turn and turn over my behavior in my mind so many years later, I am not quite sure where to place it in the file cabinet of what I know of "self." I am tempted to blame the fact that I had a bad head cold the whole trip, which certainly impacted my spirit of adventure and curiosity. I could also attribute it to the fact that I had put off two graduate school papers until the last minute, so I was having to write them in the hotel lobby in the early mornings, which meant I was tired all afternoon and at night. I could alternately point to the very real and lucky truth that my life at home was so rich at that time. In my tiny Washington, D.C., basement apartment and the four-block radius around it I had everything I needed to never leave home again: a dog, a boyfriend, my three best friends as neighbors, work that felt meaningful and challenging. Looking back, perhaps I hadn't wanted to go anywhere. Perhaps there are spans of life for travel and spans for home, and never the twain should meet. My behavior, in a childish way, was also an enormous credit to my family, for despite the fact that I had only the worst of myself to offer during that trip to Japan, I knew that they would love me through it and through it and through it again.

My mom came out of Japan Air a few minutes later with a smug, gleeful look on her face and said, "Guess what." It turned out that right after I screamed, the Japan Air employees all bee-hived around my mother, saying, "Your daughter, she is sick!"

And my mom claimed that story without question. In a mother's voice of purest certainty, she locked eyes with them and said, "Yes! Exactly. Yes. Very sick. Incurable."

And the employee who had been helping us said, "We will find a sooner flight." She found one for the next day. We had our bags all packed, we said goodbye to John, we slept that night in a Tokyo hotel, and then we three got on a plane the next day and went home.

The Gift

1

It seemed there were a few ways to go into adulthood. One was to ride all the uncertainty and relish its freedoms, laughing at the cliff's edge. The second was to fear the uncertainty and stay safe to the path, like Red Riding Hood if she had listened to her mother and never met the wolf, and to look back and wonder, *was I actually ever twenty?* I seemed more suited to this second type.

But then it occurred to me that there was a third way: skip it. Get a lift to another decade by attaching yourself to someone who had already been young. The person I tried out this idea on was fifty-six. He said his first name was a gift only for the women he slept with. On his business cards, his name read G. Christian Malaterre. He went by the nickname Chris.

I was twenty-six. My best friend at the time, Taima, warned me against him. Taima was descended from Nez Perce chiefs, and she always dated men who were tame in mind and small in body. I come from engineers and lawyers and have always loved men who were out of my control.

Her family as she knew it disintegrated when her mother died of cancer and her father left for a simpler, healthier, younger woman. From age thirteen on, she had mostly fended for herself. Thus, in her adulthood, she chose safety. She had seen her parents' world fall apart enough times for her philosophy to be *follow the procedure*. Not mine. Mine was *let's hitch a ride to some other time or place*.

The night we shared in Portland with Chris Malaterre showed the facts of our lives and of our philosophies glaringly, in unforgiving light, and it changed us both. I see now all the things I might have missed if Taima had not given me the gift she did that night.

2

That summer, Taima's life looked very different from mine, even though we had graduated together with the same degree. She had taken the first job she had been offered. She had taken the first man, too, that she reconnected with when she moved home—her best friend from seventh grade, still as blond as he had been at thirteen, still as gentle. Much wealthier, though: he worked with computers and had ridden the technology wave of the Pacific Northwest. I knew that for her, the only regrettable part of being involved with this boy was his innocence. He followed her lead in every way. When she took him to bed three days after their first lunch together, she found that he was a virgin. She doubted her ability to remain interested in someone whose entire oeuvre of sexual appeal would be things he learned from her.

My friendship with Taima was based on a few solid pillars. We both knew that sad underwater feeling of feeling mute when nervous, even among close friends. For both of us, safety lay in being able to speak. We both had fallen hard in the past for younger men, resulting in similar forms of paralyzing heartbreak. We both had been betrayed by women, including sisters, and we both felt uneasy in groups of three. Generous gifts caused us both suspicion and great guilt. We both felt cowed by all the options for how we might live our lives, and we both felt anxious about it rather than excited—we wanted to fix the corner pieces and see how the puzzle would turn out.

At twenty-six, I was a writer who masqueraded as an academic, a law firm researcher, and a host of other jobs. I invited to lunch adults who had it figured out, wanting to hear their wisdom and points of view. Most suggested practicing law instead of pursuing the gentle poverty of academia or the desperation of the writer's life. The conversations all sounded alike. Then I invited Chris, and my safe, legal, sensible universe tumbled gloriously and incomprehensibly to the ground.

He wanted to know everything. Why I had moved to this city, whether there was a boyfriend. I had shaken my head. "How interesting," he had said, over and over.

Rather than giving me advice, he poured forth his own lostness.

He was one of those men who had way of making women feel like the sole lucky recipient of the stories of his sorrow. He acknowledged that, throughout his life, women had felt protective of him, singled-out and chosen to help; one of his gifts, he said, was to make people feel special. He talked openly about therapy, past girl-friends, and things in life that had disappointed him. His main disappointments were that his marriage had ended and that he was a lawyer and not a professor. These were not secrets to him, just part of the story.

It was clear he was nervous around me. A scared animal. This part was new to me. I didn't yet know that scared animals bite.

"Until now, dear"—he always called me dear—"I have only dated women of my own age. Give or take a few years."

"Me too!" I insisted. *Me too!*

"Why you could choose me over the others . . ." he mused, squinting at me as if trying to see something he hadn't yet seen.

I spent much of our time together reassuring him. This did not seem like a problem because it seemed to mean he must like me enough to feel insecure. I didn't understand until years later, when I finally married a secure man, that insecurity is not a trustworthy trait in a lover. It meant that the man felt afraid and, like all frightened animals, would be ready to flee at any moment and save himself at all costs.

3

Because of the vastness of the difference in our ages, and the smallness of the city where we lived, this man and I had resisted being in public together anywhere other than restaurants. Once, he invited me to his house and piled upon me wifely information, such as what he ate for breakfast, and how he liked his house cleaned and by whom, and whether he dressed to the right or the left—something that I now understand because I have a son. He told me dozens of ordinary and intimate things. He unveiled his pool table and we played a game. He won. We played another game. He won again.

A week later we spent a chaste but vulnerable night together, talking about every single thing. I think, looking back, that he was afraid of my innocence. Thunder surrounded the room where we lay quietly in bed.

For the weeks that followed, I rose to wifely heights. I bought salmon, olives, scallops for dinners we had planned to cook together, all the while half-waiting for him to cancel. He usually did. When I called to see if he was coming, he would say that he was already in bed, too tired to get out.

I ate the scallops. Put the vegetables in the fridge. I would throw them away in the morning.

I waited for him to realize how lucky he was. It wasn't working. Finally, I grew tired of this game. Chris intuited that he was losing me, and so in August he invited me to meet him in Portland on a business trip. I said yes for two reasons. I wanted to hold his hand in public. I wanted to see Taima.

She was far enough away, safe; her judgment could not harm me and would not follow me home. We would be on vacation: "What happens in the Caymans stays in the Caymans!" as the shirts say. I wanted to sample the feeling of having my family meet my boyfriend, and this friend was as close to family as I dared introduce.

As I flew solo to Portland, a sentence played ring around the rosy in my mind, something Taima had said when her dad left when her mom was sick: "Always the broken people want to break the unbroken ones."

4

We ate at a restaurant called Cleandro; restaurant critics had praised its "dazzling geometry of flavors" and declared it "the most delicious mortgage payment you will ever make."

Chris had money and age, which together gave him a power that he seemed boyishly delighted to wield. He ordered two dozen oysters and two bottles of cabernet. At a triangular oak table next to the window, we three made each other laugh. I noticed several things at once.

First, I noticed that even in a city far from home, women of all ages noticed Chris. The waitress, women at other tables, even women walking on the sidewalk earlier that evening all looked at him hopefully, bashfully, as if waiting for him to acknowledge that they too, were lost souls.

Second, Taima disapproved—she thought we were a bad match—but she was prepared to enjoy the evening nonetheless.

Third, Chris noticed that Taima disapproved, and he leaned toward her all evening, trying to charm her, watching her with nervous eager eyes, even while I held his hand over the table.

Four was that I was holding his hand, rather than he holding mine.

Fifth, I noticed that I was falling into muteness; they were carrying the conversation, and I felt anything I could claim as charm beginning to evaporate.

A tuxedoed waiter had delivered a birthday cake to an elderly couple sitting a few tables over, and he bowed while they were blowing out the candles. But the candles wouldn't snuff, and so the waiter kept uncrumpling from his bow and then folding back down. The couple blew and blew but the candles were too many.

I laughed, and in the sound of my laugh, I realized that the wine was beginning to work. Taima and Chris stopped talking and turned sharply.

"What is it?" Taima asked, but I shook my head.

"She has no end of mysterious jokes with herself," Chris said, rolling his eyes slightly and refilling both of our glasses.

Taima asked, "Are you okay?"

I nodded, and she took my word for it.

Chris turned to Taima and finished a sentence: ". . . so anyway, you can't ask mothers to be discreet. Nearly let the cat out of the bag. Holy smoke!" he finished. Then he changed subjects abruptly and asked if she went to therapy. "I see a therapist twice a week," he added invitingly.

Taima leaned in and said yes.

"I swear by it," Chris went on. "I think everyone should go."

The server opened a third bottle of wine. The restaurant had grown louder as the dinner crowds kept up, and so Chris and Taima leaned toward each other. She was smiling at him in a way that I had seen before, a way that would pull men under her spell, make them trust in her bounty of gifts to make them whole again. Therapy lasted them through the remainder of the meal. I excused myself for the ladies' room once, twice.

I emerged confusedly and bumped into a waiter who led me by the small of my back to the table where Chris waited, his legs crossed, looking amused. He appraised the waiter and finally said, "Thank you for bringing back this girl. I thought I had lost her."

The waiter was humble, servile, kind. He said, "Nonsense. I found her looking for you."

Then dessert came, and Chris kept asking, and Taima kept opening. It was exactly how he did it with me at our early summer lunches, even to the same questions.

5

We had been having dinner for three hours, and Chris hadn't said a word to me for over two. My bewilderment evaporated into anger at the thought that I had already forgiven him once that day. Chris Malaterre, fatigued from his meeting and flight, gave me the wrong room number when he gave me the key.

After trying several times to get into the room, I went down to the lobby. The woman at the desk asked in a pinched librarian voice, "So you need the key because you are his . . . ?"

I had started to say "girlfriend," then "friend," and then from some guttural place the word "mistress" surfaced to my mind, making me feel sick. I thought of lying and saying "niece," or even "daughter."

"I'm his—" I stopped, then said in a voice like stepped-upon leaves. "I don't know what I am."

The woman took pity and turned kind, checked on the room, and led me up the elevator to the right room, disapproving of me all the way up. She did get excited briefly that the room had a view of the park. I looked out the window. The park was a tiny unimpressive stamp of green, the size and shape of my smallest fingernail.

I could forgive Chris because of his lostness, his myriad insecurities and failed life attempts that he had piled upon me and asked me please to hold. I could not fault him for his interest in Taima. I could tell that he felt charming, which he so often doubted his ability to be.

So I sat back and listened, hating my anger and helplessness.

They were talking about me as if I wasn't there, as if I were their pet or child. Taima was laughing as Chris said, "When I first met her, I thought she was nothing special. A skinny Ivy League honey. But you know she's stronger than either of us." Taima nodded gravely, flushed with the wine and the inclusion in his "us."

Then Taima looked at me, and all at once I knew that she envied me. And at the same time, I envied her: my life lacked a story, lacked the hurts that bonded her so fluidly to Chris. For so many hard facts of her life, I had only almosts.

Now Chris was talking about gifts. When did the talk turn that way? Where was I, and where had I been? He was saying, "I've been given awful gifts. Gifts like a monogrammed lampshade with a rooster underneath. But also, I've been given awful gifts that taught me something." Taima was nodding and nodding, and nodding and nodding some more, to try to let this man know that she understood.

Taima excused herself to the bathroom. Silence fell at our table without her. I would not be the one to speak first. I would not. *This will not work*, I thought then with a shimmering sense of truth, like the opaqueness of an oyster's inside shell. I would probably have to wade through it all, my boots in the mud, for the next thirty years.

We waited for Taima to return, so words could return. So Chris would have something charming to say.

Just as we saw her emerge, Chris took my hands in his and leaned forward as if he might whisper something. "Do you mind," he asked, "giving me her number?" When I said nothing, he asked, "How are you, dear?"

I didn't answer that either, for only one answer felt true: I felt like a call girl who'd been paid for by oysters, dearly.

6

I had lost count of how many bourbons we had all had, and I had tried once and failed to tell a story about bourbon that, I think, was supposed to be funny.

The server brought yet another dozen oysters. I had no idea who had ordered them.

"What do you read?" Chris asked.

"Some science writing, now," answered Taima, putting horseradish on an oyster. "My boyfriend, Neil"—here she mentioned him for the first time—"loves science fiction, and so I'm trying to get into the factual side of it."

"How sweet of you," said Chris. He turned abruptly to me, as if only just noticing. "How are you, darling? Enjoying those oysters?" Without waiting for an answer, he turned back to his efforts to charm my friend. "Since you are into science, do you know how they test spaceships?"

Taima shook her head.

Chris leaned in. "They break them. Every single spaceship they make, they break."

"Why?" we both asked at once.

"It doesn't do them any good to know that they don't break down here, because they can't conceive of what could happen to them up there." He pointed toward the restaurant's scalloped ceiling. "So they push every spaceship to the breaking point in order to see how much it can stand. Poetic idea, isn't it?" He grinned boyishly.

I had had enough. "Yes, it is," I said, standing. "Excuse me."

"Excuse me, too," said Taima, as she stumbled to her feet.

She was drunk, drunker than I had ever seen her. She was the tallest woman in the room, her face flushed unnaturally; her drunkenness showed. I was drunk, too, but in an angry way that made me feel soberer and judicious. Paired like puppets, we picked our way through the labyrinth of tables to the ladies' room. The bathroom was some pink female fantasy, lurid lipstick-colored quartz on two of the walls, glassed-in high heels caged atop each toilet. In the bathroom, she asked "Are you okay?" five times, then tried to hug me. When she did, she lost her footing and fell, pinning me against the mirrored wall. Taima swayed. "You're acting—strange."

"Yes, I'm fine," I said. "Please hand me a towel."

"He's not a bad man," said Taima, "Only I'm worried about you. Because. Friends. Worry."

She leaned into me and I felt myself struggling like a wild animal against the bathroom wall. "Let me go!" I cried out at last.

"Don't worry, it's okay," said Taima over and over, clutching my arms so that I could not move. "He's not bad, just don't hold his hands so much. Let him be free, let him gesture. You hold him back by holding them. He is not a bad man. It's okay."

She was wrong, I thought, my once-wise friend had fallen just as I had, and she was wrong about him, just as I was. He was too old, too unhappy, too desperate. He would hurt us both if given the chance.

"It's not okay," I told her. "You can see that it's not okay. I'm going to pay for our drinks, and then let's leave. Please let us leave. Don't order any more bourbon, please. He won't want to leave until he sees that you are ready."

"You can't pay for our drinks," said Taima, looking frightened and confused.

"He already paid for dinner, and that cost a lot. He shouldn't also pay for drinks."

"Then let's split it. Is that better?"

It was all too much to think about in the bathroom. "Let's go back to him," I said.

We returned to the table. Chris had finished his bourbon and was folding his napkin into perfectly creased triangles. "Another drink?" he asked politely, looking from one of us to the other.

"Not for me," I said.

"Me neither," said Taima.

"Are you sure? We're all taking taxis. Why don't I order one more round, and you can drink as much as you want and leave the rest?"

Taima looked helplessly at me.

"No, thanks," I said again, coldness rising through my voice.

Taima didn't say anything, and so Chris asked her about her plans for a future with Neil and she began uneasily to talk again. The server came by again, and Chris nodded at her. I shook my head. She looked briefly confused, and then returned with two more bourbons which she set onto the table. Chris tasted his bourbon and asked to taste Taima's.

I tried to remember the last time I had been this shaken by something, this uneasy and smoldering with wonder-terror that something unimaginable was about to happen. I thought of the things that had scared me in the past. The image that surfaced was a memory of myself at seven, running across my parents' lawn and feeling petrified that I might trip and fall and bite off the tip of my tongue. This had been one of my great fears as a child, probably because it was said to have happened to one of my older neighbors. I loved to run, had always loved to run, and part of the thrill that running gave me was tinged with that terror. How strange, old fears. The thrill and terror of parting with part of yourself.

What the hell was I doing here? I wondered why I hadn't wondered it before. I wanted more than anything to be back at home, away from both these people, away from this watery port-town and back in a place where boundaries ran thick and things that did not belong together stayed apart.

I stood up and put on my jacket. Taima and Chris looked up and understood. The server came around with the final bill and presented it to me. In a swift moment of final grace, Chris took it from me and paid.

7

I lost Taima that night. Just sort of shed her as a lobster sheds skin, and she let herself be shed. That night broke our friendship but secured both of our happily ever afters.

Years later, I wondered if Taima had also felt it. The gift. Amid the confusion, some rules for adulthood had been established. One year after that strange evening in Portland that split both our summers into unalike halves, Taima married her boyfriend and invited me to her wedding, even though the tectonic rift between us had already grown beyond what an ordinary woman could leap. She would never question her marriage; shelled safely inside it, she would give birth to boy after boy after boy.

I think, in part, she flirted with him, ate his oysters, drank his wine, and sacrificed our friendship to try to stop me, to try to save me from making the mistake of staying with that man.

I think, in part, I brought him there to show her what she already had and what she deserved to avoid.

I never once looked up G. Christian Malaterre to learn what became of him. Fifteen years later, he emailed me at my university email address to ask me to edit his memoirs. He had had a bad childhood, he said. These stories were finally seeping their way out and it was very healing for him. He couldn't believe he was telling me all this, but somehow he knew his secrets were safe with me. I was special that way. Would I do it?

No, I said.

He emailed back "God bless," and that was the last I ever heard from him.

8

The morning after that oyster night, I sat on the desk in Chris's hotel room, waiting for him to pack. I was already wearing my jacket and shoes, and I had brought nothing but a small overnight shoulder bag. We had slept on opposite sides of the king bed. I felt disgusted by him, almost, not quite. But I knew the disgust would come soon.

As he packed, he looked just like any man I have seen, except, somehow, flatter.

He came over and sat in the chair, facing me. He placed his gray hands on my knees and said, "You're a gift. God bless you." His eyes were wet, but only for a moment. Then he straightened up and said, "One day I know I'm going to regret this. You, dear, are a gift that I don't deserve: if I hadn't been such a wretched man, you would be my incentive to live to be a very old man. If one of my enemies doesn't kill me first."

He searched for a handkerchief but couldn't find one. He looked in his jacket pockets, but he had given last night's handkerchief to Taima when she spilled bourbon on her dress. If he remembered, he didn't let on. I opened my bag and found my handkerchief, and I handed it to him. We got on separate planes, and that was the end.

I never did learn his first name, but I learned that you don't want to skip any of it. At best, he and I could have loved each other hidden away, like fugitives in an attic; we would not have grown old together; we would not have had children. So much life I would've never known if I had leapt over this era. I imagine each moment wrapped like a gift in its own color of memory. Some will make my heart hurt—some will make it lift. All I will wish to remember. What of this would I have missed?

None.

One day—I must've had an inkling of this on that defeated, embarrassing, hungover morning, on that stiff, sham comforter of our unused hotel bed—one day, I would be forty. One day I would meet someone who is my match, one day we would breed and I would split open like a tree and bear out young saplings, one day we would stay awake for them together, we would love them and be willing to suffer for that love; and once they are grown, once they are my age and older, one day we will age and slacken and weep out sap and die. One day, together. Between this day and one day there would be so many things.

It was a glimpse: just like the view of the park, a tiny bit of green. But it was the future, and it would be mine. I took the handkerchief back. I stood up tall, looking Chris for the last time in the eye. My bag a small green burden in my hands. The door was there, behind it the entire world. I would open it.

The Steely Edge of the Universe

IN MY late twenties, when I was living alone in an apartment near the university, I developed a relationship with J & P Towing Company. Twice in one month I called them to tow a car out of my reserved parking spot. Street parking filled up each morning by seven a.m., and signs threatened to tow anyone who dared leave a car in the wrong place.

After my first call to J & P, the tow-truck driver confused my building's address and ended up a half-block short, following a car into a gated parking complex. I saw him go in, then immediately my phone rang.

"Miss McKetta?" a boy's tentative voice asked.

It turned out that the gate had closed and he and his tow-truck couldn't get out. After making several phone calls, including one to the manager of the gated parking complex, I saw the tow-truck driver outside my window. He looked about nineteen, and he explained that he had escaped by following a car out.

I had to sign a form saying that I gave consent to remove the blue Chevy pick-up from parking spot 102.

After I did, the driver, whose name was Elian, clamped locks onto the back tires of the truck and hoisted it up. I watched as it pitched off down the road.

I AM familiar with the proceedings of towing, having been to a towing lot twice: once to rescue my own car and once to help a friend rescue hers (which had been taken from my parking lot). Both times were battering experiences. The first time was in Boston. The burly money-taker at the tiny towing office laughed at me when I wanted to check that my car hadn't been damaged in the tow, and then he closed the gates so that when I checked I wouldn't be able to drive away. The laughter/lock combination puzzled me—the laugh implying that I was a trifling person to ask such questions, and the lock that I was a serious threat to his business and a possible criminal. The first time cost $150. The second time, in Austin five years later, the price had risen to $198. In cash, of course. Towing companies always require cash payment. I split it with my friend, since her car had been taken from my lot.

I asked if someone had called it in, but the woman working the desk said vaguely, "J & P is commissioned to patrol the campus area."

"Commissioned by whom?" I asked.

"Your friend was illegally parked," she answered, swerving around the question.

By the time my friend and I paid and left, the woman had offered me a job working for J & P, since I had seemed so interested in how the towing process worked. I thanked her but explained that I was in graduate school, which, by the look on her face, didn't seem to answer *her* question.

The worst part wasn't the paying, I realized both times, though the price of the towing was steep. The part that demoralized me most was having to get a ride out to the steely edge of the universe where all towing companies have their headquarters—past the airport, in parts of the city where grass hardly grows and houses are too far apart from each other, and Dr. Pepper cans, newspapers, and Dixie cups litter the road shoulders liberally because nobody is invested enough in this area to keep it clean. It is the blank between communities, the black hole (which every city has) whose barren streets etch the sad edges of maps.

It is a terrible feeling to go out to this place to reclaim a part of yourself. The car, a hostage whisked away in a game of urban ransom. Granted, a car is not such a valuable hostage as a spouse would be, or a child, sibling, parent, friend, or pet. But seeing it alongside all the other misbehaved cars parked in moody rows, seeing my cheerful red Volkswagen bug among these other derelicts, feels like picking up an innocent child from prison. The prison effect is amplified by the lot's design, a barbed wire crown along the top of the sturdy chain link fences guarding the hundreds of towed cars.

I₮ WAS mostly my fear of having my own car taken again for ransom that made me twice ransom someone else's. If tow trucks patrolled lots such as mine, and if their victim had to be either someone else's car parked in my spot, or my car parked, as a result, in someone else's spot, in terms of the time and money and sheer depressingness involved, I'd rather it not be my car. The first time I called J & P to have someone towed, I was shaky and traumatized by the violence of my action. I spent the hours before the tow truck arrived sitting with my dog and looking out the window, too nervous to work, too watchful of my own car, which I had parked behind the errant Chevy. I was fearful that I might also be towed, or that after I towed him, the owner of the Chevy might come looking for me. This was Texas; ordinary citizens were armed. And what would I deserve? What kind of louse tows people? I felt paralyzed with guilt, annoyed at the wasted afternoon, and angry at all the city-growth/high-pricing that forced this situation and the way it left me feeling. This was no longer the gentle city of my childhood; nor, apparently, was I the same harmless child.

The second time I towed someone from my spot, the owner of the car was clearly female. The car, a taupe Saab, had a flower-shaped car deodorizer hanging from the rearview mirror, a Swiffer mop in the backseat, and several small pairs of shoes cast about the floor. I parked in the next spot over (which I felt pretty certain belonged to an empty apartment) and left a note behind the windshield wipers asking her to move her car. But after an hour I was paralyzed again with fear of being towed—what if the spot where I was parked did have an owner and they came back and wanted to park? I couldn't go anywhere or concentrate on anything, so finally I dialed J & P.

I recognized the woman's voice. She was the same dispatcher of tow-trucks I had called for the Chevy just two weeks before, the same woman who had offered me the job. I explained the situation, adding that I felt guilty towing a second time, and that I had left a nice note and perhaps the taupe Saab would move of its own accord.

"I have a truck in the area," the woman finally interrupted. "I can have him over there in twenty minutes."

"Okay," I said, foolishly relieved.

When Elian arrived an hour later, he knew exactly where I lived and who I was. We shook hands cheerfully. It was eleven a.m. on a Monday, a class day, and students were walking all over the parking lot, past Elian and his tow-truck and me, signing the form. As a graduate student living six blocks from a college campus, I was about eight years older than most of my neighbors. Normally this did not bother me, but on the occasional Friday or Saturday night I felt like the weird old person, the old-young woman walking around in running clothes and dropping real letters into the blue postal box, who turned her lights out early and whose crotchety dog didn't get along with other people's dogs. That Monday morning, not only was I the weird old person, but suddenly I was also the one who was chummy with the driver of the tow-truck.

PHILOSOPHICALLY, I think, I lean socialist. Or perhaps Buddhist, or at least in the Henry David Thoreau direction of "you build things, you use them for a while, and then you pass them on." I believe that things should belong to the people who love them. I have few belongings, but the belongings I have are lovely—in those days, a condo near the University of Texas, a red VW Beetle, some pretty dresses, teacups, and a vast and unordered collection of books. But still I find myself willing, always, to give up these things, to lend anthologies to friends who I know will forget to give them back, to offer scarves to people who visit and love the scarf that I'm wearing. I have long understood that to be portable, you must free yourself of private property and its endless tentacles of attachment. If my condo had caught fire, perhaps as revenge wrought by one of the people I'd towed, I would have grabbed my laptop under one arm and my dog under the other and felt grateful to have escaped. I can always start fresh somewhere new, accumulate new dresses and books and teacups. This would be fine.

So why would sharing my parking spot cause me such philosophical worrying, such intense self-doubt? I like to think of myself as fundamentally a good person, someone who tries not to hurt or inconvenience others, someone who is loyal and understanding and, in the necessary ways, forgiving. Is it because I am so frightened of the law, of having my own car taken, that I would rather turn in someone else than be turned in myself? In the classic game theory question, the Prisoners' Dilemma, two prisoners are placed in separate cells and ordered to confess their crime. Like in all good stories, each prisoner is given three possible outcomes: You can stay silent, and if the other prisoner stays silent too, then you both will be released in several months. Or you can turn in the other prisoner and walk free, leaving the silent other with a ten-year jail sentence. But—and this is the catch of tattling—if the other prisoner turns you in too, then you are both bound to serve five years.

In a perfect situation, the answer is to be quiet and neighborly and deny that either of you did anything wrong. But if you do this, and the other prisoner turns you in, then you are saddled with ten years—similar to how two of my neighbors were saddled with $198 towing fees through my actions. To save oneself, in this society, there is a built-in incentive to betray unknown others.

BOTH TIMES, I balked when Elian handed me the towing consent form. I knew it was cowardly, but I didn't want either car owner to know that I was the person behind the tow. The second towing day, after I had asked several anxious questions about the form I had just signed, Elian explained that all towings require a signature.

"But what about the ones that happen when you are patrolling the area?" I asked.

Elian looked confused. "Patrolling is illegal," he said. "We only come when somebody calls us."

After saying goodbye to Elian, I felt heavy with disappointment both in myself and in my neighbors. How could we live this way, as people in so many transient modern living arrangements do, never knowing each other or knocking to say hello? If I had known any of these people, I might have said, "Hey, I'll be out of town for two weeks. Let your friends know that they can park in 102." If any of them had known me a year ago, they would have asked my friend to move her car instead of sending us in the middle of the night to J & P. But no such sentiments exist in cities among people who are neighbors for nine months, at best. What are nine months, after all, in the long run? You can't grow much of a garden. You can't really know a person or come to trust them.

But you can have a baby in nine months. You can complete a year of college. You can do a person a kind turn, or an unkind one.

Several hours after the second towing, I found the note I had left on the taupe Saab behind my car's windshield wipers. On the reverse side, in red handwriting, my neighbor had written:

> I apologize for parking in your "Reserved" parking spot. Unfortunately, someone parked in my spot and instead of punishing them with a $198 towing charge I parked elsewhere. I am sorry it was your spot I parked in. If this happens again, which I assure you it will not, could you just ask me to move my car? Thanks.

She didn't sign her name. I had no idea what her name even was, or where she lived. I removed the note, and went off to class and on with my day. That night I rode my bike to the gym but found that my bike lock had broken. I did not want to risk having my bike stolen, so instead of going for a swim I called the man who would become my husband, and talked to him in the darkening evening, the time of day which Hollywood producers call magic light.

I told him about my day. I told him about towing. He said that I had paid for the parking spot and absolutely done the right thing. I told him that I felt like an abominable person. He disagreed; he doesn't traffic in self-doubt the way I do, which is one of the many, many things I love about him. I said I felt the world we live in is an arms race, a tow-or-be-towed world. Perhaps, he said, and I could hear him wearying of this conversation. I said that I wanted to write the Saab owner a note apologizing and saying that if I had known who she was and where to find her, I would have found her. He agreed that it might clear my conscience.

In the center of the university, I got off the phone. I leaned my bike, unlocked, next to the Starbucks fence. I went inside and bought a twenty-dollar gift card. I considered making it $198, but that seemed like an awful lot of coffee for someone I didn't know, someone who—for all I knew—didn't drink coffee at all. On the envelope I apologized in green ink and, after some consideration, signed my name. I slipped it behind her windshield wipers. We would not be friends, but we could at least be neighbors.

Moist

WHEN MY daughter was born we had to go straight to the Neonatal Intensive Care Unit, because breathing was harder for her than it should've been. She had an IV in her hand, and when it wore out after a day, they put it in her other hand. Then her foot. Then her other foot. I watched each part of her seven-pound, ten-ounce body turn scaly as it got wrapped with IV tape and parched by the dry air of the NICU. I wanted to rub oil onto her extremities. I wanted to touch each dry part and make it moist, but she was connected to wires and away from home, not ready for me yet.

Every part of her dried out that first week of her life: her eyes, her small inverted nipples, her fingers. Everything but her lips. Her lips stayed perfect—soft and moist.

I talked to her even when I couldn't hold her. I told her about myself, about things I had learned. I told her, one evening, about need. About how important it is to need people, not things. How not needing too many things makes a person portable, able to travel light. I told her things I learned almost a decade ago, from being addicted to chapstick.

SINCE discovering chapstick at age ten, I put it on my lips between fifty and a hundred times a day. These are real numbers, by the way, not fuzzy math. I had to keep chapstick with me at all times: I had vanilla in my glove compartment; Nivea rose in the pocket of whichever boyfriend I was dating; Body Shop strawberry next to my bed; Rachel Perry banana-coconut in the kitchen; and my favorite of all, Montana huckleberry in my purse—that one I always ordered in bulk, in case I ran out.

Jump forward eleven years. I had just graduated from college. I used the first paycheck of my first writing job to book a trip to New York City. I packed clothes for a week, my notebook, toothbrush, and half a dozen tubes of chapstick: plain mint, gooey grape in a tub, Dr. Pepper-flavored, banana-coconut, lemon-lime, Montana huckleberry.

I stayed with my friend Helena, who was a first-year medical student, and spent my first day exploring. When Helena finished class, I met her for oysters at a little restaurant near Battery Park. I was telling her about my day when she interrupted me and said: "Hey, Liz, when's the last time you looked in the mirror?"

"What?" I asked. "I don't know. This morning, probably. Why?"

"Well," she said, "I was just wondering what's wrong with your lips."

She ushered me off to the bathroom to have a look. Both my top and bottom lip looked as if they had been burned. They had this awful blistery flakiness and had turned a bright lipstick burgundy. The corners of my mouth had cracked into sore-looking circles, sort of like the red dots on clown-cheeks.

Perhaps, I thought, I needed better chapstick. I dragged Helena out of the oyster bar and to a Walgreen's a few doors down. I bought a new tube of Vaseline lip therapy and thought that by the end of the night, the problem would be solved.

But the next morning, my lips had gotten worse. When I got up for breakfast, Helena was sitting at her kitchen table, practicing her sutures on a piece of raw chicken, and still she looked at my mouth and said, "Gross."

In addition, she began trying to diagnose me, telling me all of the things it "might" be—such as oral cancer. "That's what it looks like," she said apologetically. "Oh, I hope it's not Squamos cell carcinoma! Or worse . . . what if it's syphilis? If it is syphilis, you'd better treat it—untreated syphilis can lead to blindness. Or you might have Steven-Johnson Syndrome. That wouldn't be too bad—except that it's untreatable."

I still thought the problem was as simple as my needing more chapstick, so I went out and bought something stronger, with soothing herbs and lavender.

But this new chapstick didn't work, either, and my face was getting worse; the cakey redness was spreading down toward my chin and up toward my nose. So I cut my trip short and went home that day. As I took the subway back to my apartment, I noticed tactless people—mostly children—staring at me. It was disconcerting.

THAT EVENING, I had had enough. I had two more weeks before my college health insurance ran out, so I gathered every chapstick I owned and frog-marched myself to University Health Services. I wasn't sure which floor to go to. Was this an Ear, Nose, and Throat Problem, or simply Dermatology? Should I go to Sexual Health, or the Cancer Center? It turned out that all of the different wings closed at five p.m., so any problems afterward were considered Emergency.

So I waited in the University Health Campus Emergency Center, sitting among people with broken limbs, debilitating coughs, and mysterious silent ailments that did not betray themselves. I waited a long time.

Finally I got called back. The doctor looked exhausted, like those interns you see in movies who haven't slept for the better part of a week. "Well?" he said. "What is the problem?"

I explained about my mouth.

"Did you try chapstick?" he asked.

"Yes!" I said. "About twenty different kinds!" And I opened my purse, and out spilled plain mint, gooey grape in a tub, Dr. Pepper-flavored, banana-coconut, lemon-lime, Montana huckleberry, and dozens of other kinds that I had tried and that had failed me.

The doctor wanted to know how long I had been using chapstick.

I told him eleven years.

Then he asked: "How many times a day would you say you use it?"

I decided to give a conservative answer. "About thirty," I said, casually. "Give or take."

"Thirty!" he said. "Jesus." It dawned on me then

that this had to be serious, as the doctor probably wasn't supposed to say "Jesus" in front of patients.

He put on gloves and examined my mouth. He took a culture. He left the room and returned a few minutes later, and said: "The problem is that you are addicted to chapstick." He went on to say that my lips had stopped producing moisture, and that the only way to fix this was for me to go cold turkey.

I told him that that wasn't an option. I asked, "Can't you send me home with, like, a prescription or something? What is normally done in these cases?"

He gave me a scornful look. "We don't see a lot of chapstick addicts in the emergency room."

But he disappeared again and returned with a sample tube of steroid cream, the kind you use for athlete's foot. "You may put the cream on your lips twice a day. No more. If you come back here in a week addicted to this cream, I will refuse to see you." Then he left the room for good, leaving me surrounded with colored chapstick tubes poking in all different directions.

It was a sad walk home that Saturday night, but I stopped at a trashcan in Harvard Square, surrounded by punky teenagers and homeless people, and I summoned the courage to empty my purse. Down went plain mint, gooey grape in a tub; down went Dr. Pepper, banana-coconut, lemon-lime. Down went all my chapstick, including Montana huckleberry.

THERE IS an invisible line dividing before and after in most addictions, and even in such a ridiculous one, the line existed.

The things I couldn't do until my lips healed included kissing (when I tried to kiss my boyfriend, he refused because he said I was "scaly"); eating spicy food; taking big bites of any food; and using lipstick. I learned this last rule a month after the initial flare-up, when I tried to test the doctor's orders by using moisturizing lipstick—and I ended up, once again, with starchy clown-lips that took another month to heal.

But soon I learned that there were also things I *could* now do: for example, swimming. I used to have to stick near the sides of the pool or the lake, because even in the water I needed to have fast access to chapstick. But now when I went swimming with friends, I could swim out farther. I could also travel more lightly, since I no longer needed to carry a purse to tote around all my chapsticks. I could just stick money and keys in my pocket and go.

And it made me wonder: what other things did I think I needed that I could give up?

First on that list was the boyfriend. He was a place-holder—good company but certainly not the love of my life—and also I could not get him to stop using the word "irregardless," which is not actually a word.

I thought: I don't need him.

Then I realized how many belongings I had that I didn't need. That year after college, I started giving them away. If I wasn't using something well, I felt that the thing should go to somebody who would love it.

I moved into a smaller apartment. I looked at my life and all its commitments—did I truly need to be a member of this club? Was that friend actually a good friend? Did I need this job, or was I just wasting my time and keeping it to feel safe? I reexamined every thing, every person, and every commitment that I had. And I consciously chose to either keep them or let them go. I began traveling lightly in a whole new way, choosing to focus my time and energy only on the things that mattered to me.

And that's how chapstick became a divider between my teens and my twenties, an addiction that I left behind in one decade to move, un-addicted, into the next.

Teeth

1

The phone down, I went into the green-painted closet beneath the stairs with all the glow stars to wait for the call from my husband.

When it came I didn't cry—I was all cried out—but instead I lay down next to my two-year-old daughter. Sensing I needed something, perhaps a form of rescue the size of a baby, she placed her own doll in my arms before bustling off to the next thing. "Thank you," I said. A plastic baby is nothing compared to a warm fur thing, but still it was a comfort: it reminded me why we did what we did.

I pulled myself off the carpet and went to make us both tea.

It was October. Harvest time, time to pull in safely what belongs at home. Soon the full moon would rise. We had had the windows open all day. The house smelled like chai tea, like fresh leaves, with still just the slightest scent of caged mammal.

2

I had tried. For the months, years, the full decade before, I had tried one thing and then another to gentle out this creature, this dog that I had raised and loved and been unable to control.

First, we tried a dog trainer. She assessed the situation and decided that we needed to give Goblin a picture of the duress she put other dogs under, and so we should keep her in a closet every time she barks, and each time she attacks another dog, we should do the thing she hates most. What is that, the trainer asked.

"What?" I said.

"The thing your corgi hates most."

"Probably the vacuum." It was the only thing that came to mind. Aside from other dogs, Goblin pretty much liked everything.

"Okay, then," the trainer said. "Each time she bites another dog, you put her on the ottoman and vacuum her."

We fired that dog trainer, who I later learned sold her business and moved to Hawaii.

We found another—a bona fide dog psychologist who was paid as much as a pedigreed human psychologist to figure out how family pets can improve their temperaments.

This woman, Jennifer, knew what she was doing. Before she would even meet me, I was asked to fill out twelve pages of information about Goblin: her health, basic stats, and then a description of every aggressive incident that had occurred *in her life*. There was space for twelve, but those spaces only took me to her second year. At Jennifer's facilities, she put Goblin through tests. She gave Goblin a bowl of canned junk dog food. ("Sort of like a McDonald's hamburger for dogs," she said.) Then she poked at my dog with an extendable metal arm with a rubber hand at the end, trying to push her food bowl away. Naturally, Goblin snarled. "Food possession issues," the dog psychologist murmured to herself.

The next test involved other dogs. Jennifer wanted to see if Goblin had any preferences or aversions for particular other breeds. So I stood outside in that bright, warm morning, holding Goblin on her short purple leash while Jennifer passed by with a dozen different dogs who were staying at her training kennel. Goblin lunged at a husky. She lunged at Labradors, both yellow and black, male and female. She lunged at a dachshund, a poodle, and a yipping frail-looking terrier. "Non-discriminating canine aggression issues," I heard Jennifer murmur as she re-kenneled the terrier.

At the end of our session, the trainer gave a professional diagnosis and recommendations:

Goblin should not see any other dogs—even out the window—for two weeks.

For the next two months, she should only be walked during times of day when she won't see other dogs.

From now on, feed her by hand, one kibble at a time, to get her comfortable being handled. As she takes the kibble, use your other hand to touch her somewhere she is finicky about, like her ears or feet.

And last, change her name. She associates her name, Goblin, with aggression. All her life she's probably heard, "No, Goblin" and "No bite, Goblin." Give her a new name, one with a positive association. This last recommendation was the hardest for me to take, for I had named her when I was still a pup myself. My mom solved the problem by suggesting the name "Tidy," for whenever Goblin was at my mom's house, she tidied up her toys to protect them from my mom's dogs ("toy possession issues," I could hear the dog psychologist murmur.)

My husband and I argued more about her than about anything else—in Goblin all of our philosophies crashed: his grounded practicality, my hopefulness and idealism. In our discussions of her, fault lines rumbled and shifted in our marriage. I believed we could train her to be good if we just worked harder, and that way we could give her the life she had always enjoyed: sleeping next to me in bed, table scraps, freedom. "Freedom to bark and attack, you mean," said my husband, who felt that she was a threat who needed to be contained, and who believed that if you give a dog a table scrap, you kill any possibility of peaceful dinners.

Part of loving a dog is knowing that the dog will see both sides of life before you do. Birth, love, and death. Those are the only three stories. Where do dogs fit in? While most mothers store up love throughout the decades to lavish on their own young, I have been spending, spending. I had wasted my love on a bad dog.

3

Two nights before this day in October, we had watched a documentary about a pit bull rehabilitation program that brings fighting dogs into prisons, where the prisoners have to approach them—sometimes with poles, as the dogs are so deadly. I got excited and began to hope. "They might rehabilitate them to the level of Tidy," my husband said.

That day, our other dog, Woody, had a stomach-ache, so I made him rice. Then he lay on his bed, our daughter sprawled across him like a small blanket.

Earlier that day at the grocery store getting coffee and diapers, I thought of what a marvel it was that every person shopping has learned to live in relative peace and calm around their own species.

I had called a friend on the drive home—perhaps she could talk me out of my decision, still reversible?— but no. She said frankly that if my dog had run outside and attacked her or her dog, she would've thought I was a different sort of person than she knows me to be. I had tried to get sympathy from my writing group the week before: same thing. All the writers had neither children nor dogs; they had no interest in chaotic, fierce creatures.

A few days before, I tried to talk about dogs with a woman I met at the park while we pushed our toddlers on the swings, but before I got very far, she began to cry. She said, "I am home all the time cleaning up after three boys, walking up and down stairs with laundry. I stopped making beds, because what's the point?"

I think: how hard chaos is to live in.

"She will be grass," my husband says when he sees me arrive home in tears again. "Ants will walk on her."

4

When I got Goblin, I was twenty-two, living on my own as a graduate student for the first time, and hungry to have another soul share my basement apartment. For weeks, I had been having imaginary conversations in my head while I walked to and from French class. The conversations were with a small, squat, ottoman-shaped dog named Gobelins, pronounced the French plural way, after the metro station near all of the cheese vendors' tents: *Les Gobelins*. And I was narrating my life to her.

I found an ad in the Washington, D.C., paper for a litter of corgi puppies that were available from a Maryland bitch. I met the dogs' owner in a parking lot on the outskirts of the beltway. He had a white van with a backseat full of puppies. All of them were orange-brown, like fox kits. Three were playing nicely. One, a girl and clearly the terror of the litter, was rampaging all over her siblings, tugging on their ears and biting at their feet. "I want that one," I said.

Later, I tutored a high school boy who volunteered at the Humane Society. He listened to my Goblin story and said, "You never should've taken her home without meeting her parents. The way she was just listed in the newspaper like that, and you got her out of a van in a parking lot . . . Goblin clearly came from a puppy-mill."

In truth, I did not care. I loved her.

For two months, she used my carpet as her loo, slept in my bed, and chewed on everything from my socks to my chairs to my hands. One of my professors asked me privately about my red and bandaged hands, and only, I think, believed that I was okay when I invited her over for tea to meet Goblin. At night Goblin rolled into the crevice between bed and wall and got stuck, hiccupping. I woke to rescue her, she who was stuck and confused at the noises she was making. I remember the sleeplessness, being shocked into alertness in the middle of the night by whining: What did she need? To go outside? Food? I never learned to decipher her whines, but gradually she grew up, grew fur on her pink belly and between her toes, started sleeping, stopped chewing, learned to be housetrained. I would have done anything for her. After all, who else did she have? I was her protector. With a dog, the role never ends. They can't just grow up and go to college.

This dog and I developed a web of stories together:

There was the time we went to a dinner party hosted by a journalist friend, and Goblin came downstairs with a pair of black lacy women's undies in her mouth, held up triumphantly like a flag.

The time we stood on the Georgetown dock and watched the city workers cleaning up after the hurricane.

How she always rode in the backseat of the car of my twenties, a red VW Beetle, her body croissant-curled perfectly on the half-moon pad above the trunk.

Or how when I graduated we drove cross country to Los Angeles, where we lived next door to a masseuse and his two pet wolves, and how Goblin crouched at the base of his front door and barked at the wolves, who wanted to kill her. How somebody in that apartment building kept a parrot who could whistle the first half of the song from Gilligan's Island. How once, when we were at a farmer's market together near La Brea, a man in the crowd had a heart attack. And how, after eight weeks, we left LA and I felt the most immense relief to be taking Goblin with me back to Texas.

How we lived so happily in Austin in a 375-square-foot apartment where I wrote my dissertation and she lay on an orange fainting couch and barked out the window at all the dogs who passed by.

But as she got older the stories turned.

The time when the neighbor invited us over for tea and Goblin attacked her dog.

Or when I took a piece of chocolate away from her and she bit my finger so badly that the nail curled up and fell off and the doctor did not think it would grow back.

Or when she picked fights with my mother's dog that ended in hair-tufts and blood.

Or the time she burst out of the downstairs window of our apartment in Austin to attack a passing-by neighbor dog named Mac, and how she wound up with a deep fjord of a gash in her neck that took a year to heal. Months later, while her neck wound was still draining, Mac died of canine cancer. Goblin went on.

Or when I took Goblin to the beach, and she bullied crabs, beetles, and other dogs, but she was frightened of the tide because it was bigger than she.

Or, finally, the time when I fell in love with a man from Idaho who had a yellow Labrador named Woody, and how after one week living together and eight Goblin attacks, my husband and I decided we needed to do something about Goblin. Which led us on the dog-improvement journey that ended on that day in October.

Why did it take me so long to see what I would have to do?

I think because my fears for her overrode my responsibility to those she might harm. New to any form of responsibility, even this mothering of animals, I imagined her death over and over in every conceivable way: She is run over by a tractor at my in-laws' ranch. She picks a fight with a bigger bully than herself and loses, and I watch her break in another dog's jaws.

Always I am witness. Always she provokes it. Always it is violent. Never does she die of natural causes. Never does she die without me there.

Every death story I imagine for her involves teeth.

5

The night before she died I had several thoughts:

I want to be the kind of adult who can control her creatures.

I want to be the kind of adult who doesn't care about mess.

I want to be the kind of adult who accepts that her behavior isn't perfect.

I want to be the kind of adult who children understand.

I want to be the kind of adult whose loyalty people can trust.

I want to be the kind of adult who doesn't let a bad dog destroy her family.

There we were at bedtime, sitting pastorally in the living room, straight out of *Goodnight Moon*: there was the great green room; and the fireplace; and, scattered around the floor, my daughter's toys, including a comb and a toy mouse. Goodnight family. Goodnight, mother, father, daughter, Labrador. Where is the corgi?

Goodnight to the mighty and impudent Tidy Goblin.

6

I grow up. The dog is seven, I am twenty-nine, I am getting married, I am driving my red VW Beetle up to Boise, Idaho, where I will live: a small family town where sidewalks stay clean and good dogs sniff each other on the endless trails back behind the downtown houses. Where Tidy Goblin does not fit in, not at all. Friends who walk by with their dogs stop in for a drink and dinner. Tidy throws herself against the window, her mouth like a macerator, punch-biting at me when I grab the back of her neck and drag her away.

We live now with Woody, my husband's hand-me-down Labrador. Woody did not like sleeping next to this snaky sister, this volcanic animal that might at any time erupt, and often did, leaving him scars on his nose that he would have for the rest of his life.

Woody, I should add, is perfect. The pick of the litter sired by Ruger, the best damn hunting dog in Athens, Texas, Woody was run over by a tractor when he was eight weeks old, the same age at which Goblin came to live with me. His hip shattered, and his owner couldn't afford the surgery, so my father-in-law stepped in. "I'll take Ruger's boy," he said. This was Woody's legacy: he was the best dog of the best dog. By running under the tractor's wheels, he had lost his chance to become the next best hunting dog. So he became a ranch pet, named after a *Toy Story* character by a four-year-old girl. Woody earned his keep by being friendly. When he was a puppy at my father-in-law's ranch in Texas, he became best friends with a pair of cats who let him carry them around in his mouth, as well as with an injured goose who couldn't fly south with its flock. The goose followed Woody around for the short Texas winter, and then flew away. Woody, we would trust with anybody.

In Boise, at first, Tidy Goblin and I were a pair of misfits: she, angry and orange and ferocious on her dwarf-dog legs, and I, this wife imported but still without roots, this overeducated aspiring writer, this indoor girl who didn't know how to kayak, mountain bike, snowboard, or grow tomatoes. While Woody and my husband went for six-hour bike rides, Tidy Goblin and I stayed home, curled together on the couch or bed, reading. When Woody came home, happy and tired, Tidy Goblin usually attacked him over some bizarre and invisible thing, such as a dead caterpillar on the back deck that he innocently sniffed. We amended our already restrictive dog-systems. We began feeding the dogs separately and letting only one dog loose in the house at a time.

We bought Tidy Goblin a crate. If we let both dogs loose in the house, Tidy Goblin would bite Woody. Woody cowered during these attacks; he was too good a dog to fight back. But we knew that if he ever did fight her, he could kill her in a bite. This fear loomed, too: of Woody becoming a killer. Of losing two dogs and not just one. Increasingly, Goblin went into her crate or got stuffed in an upstairs bedroom.

Friends with well-behaved Labradors visited and would ask: "Who is that dog in the cage?"

"It's a *crate*," I responded. "And her name is Tidy."

There began to be a smell of caged mammal inside our house, the scent you remember from having hamsters or having children who kept hamsters. It is a warm fur smell mixed with cedar chip and the wetness of urine or spilled water-bowl.

And then I got pregnant. People asked if I would give my corgi up, and I told them, in only slightly less polite terms, *No, and bugger off.*

And yet I feared the Lady-and-the-Tramp-ing that comes with having children. I had seen so many aging dogs exiled. One friend with two toddlers had to euthanize her dying fifteen-year-old collie and told me that she spent the last four hours holding the dog's head in her lap, petting her and talking to her, and trying to make up for the last four years.

I didn't want that. I saw it happening to us in worse ways than what I had seen in the houses of my married-with-children friends, where their dogs at least were not a threat to their children, and their dogs didn't bite when bathed or bark savagely at the neighbors.

Two months before the baby was born, we took a trip to visit family in California. Tidy Goblin picked a fight with my sister-in-law's pit bull puppy and lost. She had to wear a cone for two weeks and have a drainage tube stuck out of her back leg. It was sad seeing her all doped up on the anesthesia, and on our walk that first night after her injury, she bumped into the curbs that were exactly her head-height and couldn't get off the road to find a patch of grass. I tried to lift her to a grass spot, but even doped up, Goblin had the dignity to snarl.

7

I am crying about Goblin again. It is six in the morning and I have a cold and my nose is a mess and when I wake in the night to blow it I worry about things out of my control. Last night was long and shaky. I would feel better if I exercised, took Woody for a short walk. I would feel better if I got to work. But I am feeling the gray-day uselessness of it. I am feeling that the world is moving ahead, too fast for me, and I just want to sit in my husband's office and be near the window. My soul feels in chaos.

I was loving, I was soft, I was all gums, I was devoted

to my animal firstborn at the expense of anything. Take it, take it, take it, I had promised this dog without words. If you want it, it is yours. I saw a daughter in her: Goblin picking up her toys; purging the world of all chaos, all other dogs.

My human daughter is so naturally orderly—always wanting the things on her shelves to be straight. Her natural order reminds me that orderliness is an element of human nature, not some drawn-on thing that we apply to ourselves. My girl is in her second week of part-time school, and when she arrived yesterday she saw her friend Caleb and then he fell down on his face. "Uh-oh," my girl said. The adults, Montessori-style, were ignoring it to let him know that kids just fall—and then they get up. My girl walked over to the teachers: "Uh-oh! Uh-oh!" At pickup, she saw my husband's fly accidentally down and said, "Uh-oh!" and ran to point it out. These things, she needed us to know, were out of order.

Today is the day, at two p.m. is Goblin's appointment. It's strange and sad to think about her today, while she's still alive. Alive for eight more hours. There is still time for something or somebody to rescue her.

8

There was a fairy-tale-in-reverse element happening that I did not like. Tidy Goblin had gone from a puppyhood of happily-ever-after, to a young dog-hood of some strife and loss of privilege, to an adult dog-hood of being locked in a tower. I hated the thought that there was no silver lining and she had used up all her "happily-ever-after." Even her name, this spliced, awkward hybrid, was a demotion.

The name was an attempt to turn over a new leaf: Leave the bad behavior in another decade, another name. Bury the bad. From now on we will all be good friends and not bite. Her name is Tidy now. Goblin is gone. We don't call her Goblin anymore.

She is smart, she gets it. She looks up when I call her by her new name. Sometimes when I miss our old life, when this castle in the fairy tale clouds that is adulthood feels at once too ample and too scrutinized, when I lose my footing between chaos and order, I whisper into her ear the first name: *Goblin. Goblin.*

She is not a good family dog, and now I am a family woman. She guards me; it is Woody who guards my tribe. When my husband and I complete a run and leave our daughter outside on the back deck asleep in her stroller, Woody lies beside her. Goblin may adore me. But what about the people I adore?

She spends her days exiled in her crate, and I cannot help but think of her as my own caged madwoman, furious at being shoved away in the attic. If I send her out of my home, I am sending a part of myself, the wild girl, pre-husband, pre-daughter, pre-responsible homeowner. I am at once forgiving of and appalled by the requisite taming that goes on inside a marriage, or inside a house, in order for a family of people to survive together.

But once upon a time she was tame. Perhaps once upon a time we all were. I remember when I first took her grocery shopping and she spent the whole hour asleep on my shoulder. When I got her, I was in graduate school studying Zelda Fitzgerald. I adored Zelda because she was so wild, so untamed, so badly behaved. Over the years I cultivated a part of myself—or perhaps cultivate is the wrong word—I let a part of myself run similarly wild—knowing that at some point, if I wanted the whole package deal of marriage-children-house, that wild Zelda part would need to be filed away. It is simply this: that part is a destructive force, and responsibility—and creativity, upkeep, and a constant writerly revision—is all necessary to make that package deal work. It is not glamorous. It is not wild. It is often incredibly tamed and tended. And yet it is joyful too, and quiet and loud, and peaceful, and wildly beautiful and inspiring.

I saw that in letting go of Goblin, I was quelling the beast in me, the beast from my life before who refused with all her might to be tamed.

After I married and had a baby, Tidy Goblin was reduced to sitting under my desk for a few hours each morning, resting while I wrote. Beyond that, she spent her days in her crate. Corgis are herding dogs. They are built, like me, to work. They like to be organized and they nip at dogs and people who get out of order. Nothing bothers Goblin quite like being at a crosswalk and having half of her people cross while the others wait on the curb. I imagine that sitting in her crate while her family's life played on in front of her eyes was one of the deepest circles of her own personal corgi-brain hell.

"I want to come back as a herding dog," my dearest, oldest friend says. "But only if I have a job."

The closer my life got to reaching its ideal state, the worse off she was. Still, we let her get worse.

9

This day, after breakfast, my daughter goes around the house kissing her treasures—her green plastic car, her book, Woody. I think of a yoga teacher who said, *We come to this earth empty-handed, and we will leave this earth empty-handed, so we have nothing to lose, nothing to worry about, nothing to fear.* My girl came into this world empty-handed but immediately found me, her mother. She clung to me against loss. Then to her father, then her blanket. Now her maracas, her shoes, her books, her dog, her little green car.

My girl now has teeth and opinions. The fighting tools. Weapons, if she ever needs them. She sharpens both against me. My tiny daughter goes everywhere with me, like Goblin used to. She entertains the adults, like Goblin used to. I know that she is watching. I know that if I behave badly, she will listen and behave badly, too. Just the way that if I unload the dishwasher, she watches and wants to hold the forks. Or the way she knows that shoes go on feet and hats on heads and that sponges are used to scrub the floor. She understands. I try to behave well, to fight fair. But while we teach our daughters how to be good, we rarely teach them how and when things need to get bloody. When to use her teeth, and when to smile and look away.

Our girl loves dogs, and because we keep Goblin away from her, it's never occurred to her that a dog might bite. Woody is her growth chart: every Monday my husband takes a photo of her next to him: first a little bundle of blankets on his dog-bed, with Woody pointedly looking away, then gradually she was big enough to lean on Woody while he patiently sat still, and now, finally, she is a walking, talking, dog enthusiast who wakes and asks for Woody-Dog (her first word, pronounced "Whee-Whee-Whee-GAH"). She drapes herself over him like a saddle on his back. When she sees or hears Tidy Goblin barking her head off in her crate, my girl simply says, "Ti-ee woof!"

I spend the morning reading my daughter fairy tales, especially the ones like Rapunzel where the girl gets out of a tower, or Cinderella where she is unearthed from the hearth to become a princess. My husband stops by our spot near Woody's bed and listens a minute, and then he points out that Tidy Goblin's life has been Cinderella in reverse: from the queen who ate *fromage* from the table and slept on the bed; to a slightly lesser member of court; and finally to the victim who spends her life in a cage. ("I've already had that thought," I told him, "and it's a crate, not a cage.") "Ti-ee Woof?" our girl says, upon hearing her name. She looks around, as if noticing for the first time the quiet.

10

I realized that every week, like clockwork, I was feeling terrible about my decision to have this dog in my house, in her current state. She was a caged mammal. Her crate was actually a cage, whatever I insisted people call it. You could see it and you could smell it, plainly. Her captivity was barnacling out my energy and my interest in my life. I found that I could not get excited about things. If being young and loving rashly is a great mountain range, the spine of a young earth, then getting older and loving with practical reservation is a flatland, a moor. I just looked up moor—it is a tract of uncultivated upland reserved for shooting.

This is a Magic Time, older parents would tell me, but I could not find peace in the days when we knew one of our creatures might at any point kill the other. "Try medication," one friend says. "It has helped me." "No thanks," I say. "Try meditation," says another. I try. But you can't meditate your way out of having a bad dog.

So I opened the door to finding her a new home. It was something that years ago, or even six months ago, would've driven me to tears.

We tried a friend who had lost a herding dog recently. She wasn't ready.

We tried a college student who I used to tutor in English who was obsessed with Cesar Milan. He already had a dog.

I tried a friend who raises corgis in Texas. She said she'd ask around.

I tried my mom, always a rescuer, who lives with a dog, a cat, and a frequently visiting second dog, all of whom get along great. She said to count her as my last resort.

We tried a corgi rescue in Idaho, where we learned that if the dog is aggressive, the correct thing to do is try to correct the aggression before re-homing—(we tried, we tried!) and if the aggression cannot be corrected, then the right thing to do is put the dog down.

This opened a new door that we were afraid to look into, but suddenly we saw some logic there. Even if we found a new home, she could still use her teeth on any other creature who got in her way. How could we pass on this corgi, a known fighter-to-the-intended-death, to another home? She would just be a time bomb, ticking.

There is always one bite that seals a dog's fate. She had so many bites, but the final one was when she attacked a tiny schnauzer whose owner showed up at the door with a note: "Can your daughter come play with my granddaughter?" And Tidy Goblin attacked, and schnauzer hair and schnauzer blood shook the air, and it would have been a death-fight if my husband hadn't come in, picked up Goblin, and set the schnauzer free from her mouth. We chased the owner down the street, saying we will pay for everything! She let us pay. Her dog lived. But she never forgave us, and I do not blame her for that.

And after that, things changed. My dog could not live in my house anymore.

It was a full moon night when I found her a new place to live. Finally, a woman who used to dog-sit for her, who bred corgis for show and sheep, said okay. Tidy Goblin would live at a house on Fox Brush Road—fitting because she looked so much like a fox, unfitting because she has no tail.

In a way, I felt that Tidy Goblin was going back to her beginning, before she was my only dog and I was her only person—she would not be special, but of a pack: she would be surrounded by her kind. By leaving her there, I was running her through that sieve that catches our harsh edges and youthful bad behavior, that prohibits us from bringing them in, that tells us, *Look, if you are going to be a part of this world, then you had better behave. No barking at the neighbors. Leave such behavior behind, as you should. Be like all the other corgis.* In the best of cases, I thought hers might be a perfectly circular story.

Her last two nights living with me I let her do whatever she wanted, short of eating my daughter—she could kick up grass after every pee, stop and sniff any patch of world that caught her attention, sleep in the bed (my husband slept those nights in the guest bed in case she woke and attacked him). My anti-scrap husband even fed her a taco! I took her for a swim in the reservoir and I didn't stop her when she rolled in poo. I gave her a bath and because she tried to bite me when I came at her with a towel, I let her dry out in the sun. Then I packed a copy of her vet records, her leash, her bed, her heartworm medicine, a bag of her food, her corgi herding certificate, and her crate.

At the Fox Brush Road house, there were two other corgis running around the front yard fence. Tidy sniffed at them but didn't bark. I said, "Goodbye." And I told her to live a long life, free and happy. I kissed her forehead. I did not say "I'll be back soon," which is what I said every other time I left her anywhere for any amount of time. She watched me for a long time through the glass door. I went back once to look at her again. She was extremely puffy from her bath from the day before. Her face was white. Her dark eyes were still watching me, waiting for a signal.

My sister-in-law had come with me, and as we got into the car she asked, "Do you need a hug?" As we pulled out of the driveway, I saw that Tidy Goblin had been let out into the yard with the other corgis. First she ran over to the fence and lifted her leg and peed like a boy. Then she wagged her tail tentatively when the other corgis came over to smell her. Then she stood at the fence for a long moment watching me. And finally, she ran up toward the house, and toward the other dogs, and out of my sight.

11

On that day in October, just before my husband left, our daughter dropped a tea mug and it broke and I said, "That happens," and all during lunch she repeated with perfect clarity, "That happens."

I felt a huge relief at shedding the lie I had told myself for years that Tidy's life was okay here. It is exhausting to lie to oneself and now that weight has gone. The night before I dropped her there, only a week earlier, Woody and I walked in the full moon light on his first ever single dog walk in the foothills, and I imagined Goblin at her new home, under the same moon, during the full-moon mammal beast hour, wondering if I'd ever come back for her.

I made scones. I folded the laundry. I made myself a cappuccino. I took care of my house and now I am just waiting. I strapped my daughter into the baby carrier and put on her white and green striped hat with a Baba doll stitched on the front, and we took Woody around the block. On the walk, I talked with my daughter about forgiveness, even though I doubted she could understand. I wondered whether Tidy Goblin's spirit in whatever form it takes will understand and forgive me and see that I felt I had no choice. How exhausting her life has been for her, and for us. It will be more peaceful, safer, here without her. But she was my protector, my guardian, even if she did a botched job. I send a silent thank you into the air to the herding dog of my heart.

12

I can't blame anyone for being the worst of themselves, because sometimes we all are. The kindest adults you meet were often the worst kids. I am a decent adult, though, according to all sources, I was not that nice a kid. I grew into myself at age eleven after a trip with my grandparents to see the Holocaust memorials in Germany and the freshly chipped away Berlin Wall. I grew into kindness, the story goes, at realizing my privilege when so many other children were put into ovens like in Hansel and Gretel, becoming ashes, ashes.

I came back home kind, helpful, no longer a sower of chaos. A true big sister.

I will go into the rest of my life having Labradors—they are big, kind, peaceful, and unopinionated. They coexist. I prized my corgi for the qualities I saw in me. She was clever. She was portable. She liked all people. She had the bad habit of biting her feet, and I have the bad habit of biting my nails. What does it mean to attack one's hands with one's mouth? Perhaps Goblin lives on in my teeth?

Parenting Goblin and Woody alongside each other gave me a perverse and unexpected sympathy for Cinderella's stepmother. She wanted to be a good parent both to her own lineage and to her husband's. But her step-daughter was *so much better than her own daughters*, whom the stepmother had raised. Squeezed them out of her own small pelvis, taught them please and thank you, fed them as babies.

You cannot feed something and then not love it.

Living with Tidy is like having a crazy person in the house, my husband said, whenever he could see me feeling too sympathetic toward the corgi.

Physically, Tidy Goblin had aged well. Her muscles stayed strong. Her teeth remained sharp. But sometimes she stared at things for a little too long. The vet thought she might have brain lesions, which are known to cause aggression. "See how she zones out, her eyes do strange things? If she were my own," the vet said hesitatingly, "I'd probably euthanize her."

Woody's was a Cinderella story, a story of a good creature rising, the true good self being seen and rewarded. Goblin's was the story, perhaps, of the evil stepsister. She represents a violent nuisance. What happens to evil stepsisters in the end? Sometimes they are granted a happy ending: Cinderella forgives them, invites them to her wedding. In other cases, they aren't forgiven, and they are punished: They die by fire, by doves pecking out their eyes, by being turned to stone. They die, euthanized with their mother's consent.

A week after I said goodbye to her forever, the corgi-breeder called and said, you need to take her back. "She bit one of my dogs and I cannot keep her."

I realized that it would be better for her to be memories and ashes, scattered in the dry grass of the Idaho hills, than alive and using her teeth. So we called the vet and made an appointment.

13

In an hour it will all be over. My husband would hold her during the injection; the vet would feed her cream cheese; we would stay here with Woody. Soon it would be done, gone. The labor of keeping, stewarding, loving this dog, gone. My young woman's labor put into her. One of my friends who loved her too comforted me by saying, "Your stress-free home life will be Goblin's final gift to you, her final act as your guardian."

There would be chaos, but not teeth. There would always be, I was beginning to discern, chaos. My toddler daughter moves fast, needs to have so many things explained—why we don't run in the street, pour our milk on the floor, bring our blankets to meals, throw our books in the dogs' water bowls. Recently she ran across a crowded restaurant, lost to us briefly, to pat a wooden dog statue on the head. But this beautiful chaos—this beauty—was my life.

I never loved her any less. I just loved my life more.

14

I had a fox-dream about her the night after I gave the command to turn her to ashes. It took place in the green hills that run north of downtown Boise, my favorite of the wild places of Idaho just outside our door. We were on a walk, just us, when another dog came running in our direction. I braced myself for violence. But, to my astonishment, she rolled over, belly-up, vulnerable and surrendering. The other dog sniffed at her and moved on. Then when she came back up again, I saw that this dog wasn't my dog after all, but a fox—her long plume-tail rose up, a red feather, a hint of her wildness. She was and wasn't Goblin.

We moved Woody's bed into our bedroom—it felt good to have him close. When my daughter stirs he stirs, too, and we go in and wake her together. The other morning, she tore naked through our rooms, giggling and shrieking, only finally to collapse on top of Woody. I watched them for the few seconds it lasted, an old white-yellow lab, the color of hominy, relaxed, happy—and perpendicularing him like the leg of a T, a long naked girl. They rested there for a long time.

There are still marks on the carpet where her crate used to be. They will go away with time.

And I remembered the first night I had Goblin—before marriage, before she was Tidy, before I was anyone's mother, before I ever believed I could've executed a decision to put anyone to death. When I was a young graduate student living in a low-ceilinged basement apartment—that night I lifted her out of her bed and held her on my shoulder, like an infant, after her first day in my life. She breathed deeply. She slept in total oblivion, her kitten-soft head on my shoulder. I wondered, briefly, if this was what having a baby was like: this longing to nurture, this lavishing of love on a small, whole thing. I had no real idea whether I'd ever do it for a human. She didn't wake, even after I lowered her gently down onto my bed, where she and I would sleep our first scattered newborn night, together.

15

Right before the appointed hour of two o'clock, my mother calls with one last attempt. But I cannot hear it.

"No," I tell my mother who loves her, too, who gave the dog gifts addressed to *my first born's first born*. "I don't want you to rescue me. I want your blessing that this awful thing I'm going to do is the right thing."

"You have it," she said without a pause.

We both waited for me to cry.

"Thank you," I said, not crying. Then we said I love you and hung up. I could not think straight—this was surely a protection—I could only think in circles, in riddles. What do you love and yet refuse life to? What are you left with at the end of any love story? What do a mother and a monk and a writer have in common?

All three have empty space inside, where new life has room to grow. All three empty themselves out, in order to honor the life that must live.

I found my daughter lying with Woody on his bed, trying to fit her Baba doll cap over his long ears.

The phone down, I went into the green-painted closet beneath the stairs with all the glow stars, to wait for the call from my husband.

Madewell

1

Whatever else my mother is or isn't, she was well-made by the forces that shaped her life, and she was determined that the same be true for me. Even when I was forty-one.

February, just before the virus struck, was the last time I ever set foot in my parents' home in the city where they raised me. I visited alone, which I rarely did.

While I was there, my mother took me shopping for a gray woolen blazer I felt sure I would never wear but that was symbolic of my mother's knowledge about essential things—or perhaps, simply, of my mother. My mother-bear mother who has abundant advice, and who believes that lines are for people who are afraid to skip them. My bulldog mother who would ferociously call the governor's office to demand a coronavirus vaccination after her doctor told her she would have to wait. My clever mother with her system-navigating genius. I've seen interviews with ancient Jewish women who used such persistence to talk Nazi guards into giving them their family back.

My mother got her way. With the governor. She usually does.

Somehow, I didn't inherit this trait.

The buying of this woolen object struck me as funny at the time, though I am still not sure if it is really a story. Like anything that happens between mothers and daughters, it's never clear what to label it. Here goes.

As soon as I arrived in Austin—before I unpacked my small solo-travel backpack into my old dresser and set up my computer so I could write mornings, both my ways of creating new routines within the old beautiful chaos—my mom called me into her closet.

She was standing among her things: her half dozen necklace holders with bright, fun necklaces, ranging from family heirlooms to wooden beads on strings. Below her was the cat's litter box, and on the wall were art and clocks. Everywhere my mother lives, she puts on the wall an endless array of clocks, all telling different times.

Not only are all the times different, but so are the clocks: one belongs in a 1950s diner; one is Humpty Dumpty, with hands ticking across the face of an egg with legs; one is gold and meant to represent communism, for its tinkering workers make the second-hand move; one is a fly-swatter with an incessant, escaping fly as the minute-hand; one is painted with a dreamy mural and has never worked.

Is the point that time is just nonsense? Is it that all of life plays out against our ticking mortality, and we must always keep watch? Or do her clocks represent the world she made for us, where time likes to play, where unless we really, really, *really* wanted to, we would never have to grow up?

On this day, my mother was taking something off a clothes-hanger and holding it up for me: a tan wool blazer, size S, from a company called Madewell.

"Try it on," she said, holding it around my shoulders. "It's a great company that your sister loves, and it's having a thirty-percent-off sale right now."

I was living, then, in a tiny house, 275 square feet—my closet was made up of eight dresses, two sweaters, two exercise outfits, and some leggings, socks, and knickers. It was no bigger or smaller than my husband's, son's, or daughter's wardrobes. In a tiny house, you think hard before bringing anything inside. In a tiny house, there is only room for you, as you are now.

My relationship with stuff has evolved in spite of and because of my mother—my closet is the same width as my hips. Still it shrinks. Friends come for dinner and leave with new boots, a purse, a black dress. I have somehow a sense that it is impossible to have few enough things. But there is a part of my mother's bounty I want to preserve, to cultivate. As a young mother, she had a generosity of time, too, that I seem to lack. Her days were open for children. Our disorder and our timeless nonsense gave structure to her days.

Even as an adult, I have often been dressed by my mother, who used to greet me when I was home from college with endless black dresses that she bought in my size. I wore them to pieces.

Now I am in my forties, and I don't like the blazer. Still, I put it on because she is my mother. It is boxy and not at all my style, but I said "nice" and gave it back.

I remember a time, twenty Christmases ago, when the same thing happened with cookies: "Do you like the amaretto biscuit from the sample tray at the café?" my mother asked. "Yeah, it's nice," I answered, untruthfully—then found a ten-pound bag of them beneath the tree, from Santa.

"Do you think this is the right size?" she asked of the blazer. "An extra-small would take away some of this extra material on the back." She pulled a handful of tan wool away from my spine.

"I think either size is fine, but I really don't need one of these. I doubt I'll wear it much."

She nodded. It was clear to her that I was wrong. While I sat on her bathroom counter and looked at her clocks, she called the Madewell store on trendy South Congress Avenue. They had a gray version of the XS blazer that they would hold until tomorrow night.

"We'll go tomorrow," my mother said to me.

2

As I was drafting this piece, my beloved mom sent me an *Atlantic* article about good advice and how it threatens parent-child relationships when grandchildren are involved. "Let me know if ever I need to change," she bravely wrote in the email. My mother, who, like any being on earth, is caught in the web between the need to be her purest version of herself and the need to evolve in order not to perish.

My mother, who has heard from all four children all versions of,

Mom, you're bugging me.

Mom, you're just freaked out that I married someone different from Dad.

Mom, stop giving me advice.

Who has watched her children step away, step away, step away.

But then the moment we need anything, we scurry home to her. Back to our old bedrooms, which she has kept for us just so. Back to her long wooden table that could have held Jesus and all twelve disciples with room for a few more.

What is it about daughters and moms in fairy tales that the girls are always lost to them?

Perhaps it is because, in life, we always are.

Here is the free advice my mother has given me, always preceded with: "free advice is worth what you pay for."

- In a relationship, it's better to be the dumper than the dumpee.
- When in doubt, go to graduate school (repeat as needed throughout life).
- In choosing a career, obtain the highest degree. Better to be a lawyer than a legal assistant. Better to be a physician than a PA. Better to get a PhD than an MA.
- However many degrees you have, stay home with your children, if you can.
- Best to have at least three children.
- Always have a dog and let it sleep in the bed.
- Drink organic milk. Wear sunscreen. Read the *New York Times*. Go to the doctor.

It is generally good advice. Ninety percent of her advice has shaped ninety percent of my life's good parts. But the remaining ten percent is generally wrong.

A nuisance. It's amoretti biscuits and Madewell blazers and giving her children a drive downtown but dropping them off on the wrong side of Lamar Boulevard.

Where to draw the line? Would it have been better to have said no thanks to the lift, and simply walked?

As I woke up the morning of our shopping trip, I wondered dizzily what time it was. All of the clocks in my bedroom said different times. The chicken clock said 4:15, which seemed the most likely. It had said 4:15 for years.

3

Often, I find my children entertaining themselves with gifts my mother has sent: how I loved finding my baby daughter sprawled naked on the carpet after the bath, reading a cardboard book from my mother with a photo of a baby eating a banana.

My mother and I both nearly cried when I emptied out my old bedroom when it was time to leave Texas after graduate school. After a lifetime of following her free advice, of being the dumper, of getting the PhD, drinking organic milk, wearing sunscreen, letting all dogs sleep in my bed. All these beautiful objects thrown away, given away to the charity shops that my mother liked to browse and buy from, adding to the bounty of her irreducible clutter. My mother expresses love through gifts, through a saturating sense of generosity. Her gifts have furnished nearly all of my houses.

Now I watch this process in my daughter, who inherited from me who inherited from my mother who inherited from our cave-decorating ancestors this need to surround ourselves with a thousand potentially useful objects.

This would be one thing for a woman who never leaves the house, who lives in one place all her life, but my mother has a nomadic heart, attuned to any rumble that might turn home into a threat. She is always ready for the next pack-and-move, prepared to abandon everything but her young. She has never needed to do this—but she remains at all times prepared.

My heart, like my mother's and my daughter's, will always be a site of clashing battles between the abundance of having everything and the fly-by-night urge to leave it all behind. Myself versus myself, down to the very ventricles.

As a young woman, my mother loved the same sorts of men that I loved: her first husband was a dark-haired, brooding doctor with a family history of suicide—a lost, broken-winged boy who flitted moth-like to the bright light of my mother's temperament. Her first boyfriend after she divorced, at age twenty-six, was a poet. He wrote poems for her. She was in graduate school: a hard, disciplined worker who treated school like a job; who gave herself one day off from studying per week, usually Saturday; who remembered what it was like to be left without money and who swore to herself she would do the work to never again go without. She would not marry the poet. Instead, she studied at the law library, where her ex-husband's younger brother introduced her to my dad. He was tall and red-haired and smiley. There was none of the brooder in him, none of the poet. He was a worker, like she, and he had a bright light of his own, to which others flitted. They would marry, breed, both get law degrees, and set up a house-hub together, where they would always be outnumbered by children and have too many pets.

Throughout my childhood, I was almost entirely my mother's daughter. We had the same coloring, the same runner's legs. We both liked people. We both loved school. Frequently I have heard her say that I was an easy teenager, which is true; I swam along in her wake because I liked the way she sailed. Her life looked like fun to me: it had a too-muchness that I admired. There were always too many dogs, too many kids crowding up the house, both her own and our friends. Too much food in the pantry and too many conflicting schedules to plan a sit-down meal. The only times I remember sitting down as a family were on holidays, with cousins and grandparents, and my grandfather saying grace while the rest of us heathens blinked and held hands. The chaos of my mother's house included too many clocks, too many coffee mugs, too many wooden chickens, too many collections that kept growing. It was a house with much play and few rules. It was a house where a part of me wanted to stay forever.

4

My mom, who sleeps later than my dad and I, woke up that morning ready. Madewell would open in half an hour, and traffic in Austin is awful. Best to go now, try it on, say yes or no to it, she said.

We set out in her car, with my mother driving. She wore a green and blue plaid flannel long-sleeved shirt. She brought for me the too-big tan blazer, in case I got cold. I wore one of my eight tiny house dresses, three of which I had packed for this weekend.

We battled the midday traffic across the bridge, talking about our classes. We are both teachers, and this is an easy default. All the parking spots were taken on South Congress Avenue except for two right in front of Madewell. My mother pulled in and said, "Thank you, Gloria!"

Gloria is my mother's guardian parking angel. Gloria never fails to find her a spot. When I moved to Washington, D.C., for two years in my twenties (for more graduate school), my mother gifted me Gloria, too, and since then I have a sort of magic for being able to find a good spot to park.

My mom was especially pumped about this, for Gloria must really want us to be at Madewell if she left us not just one perfect spot, but two. But then we realized that all the parking had to be backwards, facing out. This was going to be hard. I would've given up at that, were I the driver. But not my mom. She waited until a small traffic break, pulled out, and waved at the cars who waited.

All the other drivers wanted her spot, because that is how Austin is: how all cities are, when they grow too far from their roots, their genetic blueprints. A few drivers began to honk.

Undeterred, my mother turned the car around, taking up both lanes of inbound traffic toward downtown, and maneuvered the car backward, in a clumsy loop, until it fit, somewhat, in one of the two parking places in the correct direction. It was not inside the lines.

"Think I'll get a ticket?" she asked.

"Nah," I said.

There was still a full open spot to her left, into which the most persistent of the waiting drivers pulled. We got out and my mother thanked him for his patience.

Then we went into Madewell: boxy sweaters; heavy, well-made plaid shirts; long varieties of jeans striping tables like blue tongues of taffy. All of the other shoppers were hip Austinite women in their twenties and thirties. One was pregnant. She was wearing a gorgeous striped gray dress, tight against her belly, and I thought with a sudden flare of nostalgia about what that had been like.

5

I know my mother loved to be pregnant, did it five times, though only four babies lived; she says often that she wished she had done it once more.

I envied her feeling this way, her forgiving the rebellious body out of love for its creature. Of pregnancy I remember mostly the nausea, both times, and the publicness of the body, how compelled strangers felt to touch my belly and give advice. I had been a growly, angry pregnant woman, warding off comments by people I liked and still like, but who lost their heads entirely and said abhorrent things such as, "When are you going to drop that thing?" and "You're still pregnant?" These are direct quotes.

When I was pregnant, my mother always wanted to talk about the body. She wanted to know how my breasts felt, if I was feeling the practice contractions, what foods I craved. Her excitement that her first-born was soon joining her in motherhood had a palpability and a boiling-over quality. This makes sense, for there is nothing so physical, so body-humbling and mammalian, as having a baby. She wanted to talk about how we were alike, and perhaps I bristled at being pulled into the Mother-Camp before I was ready. It felt like one more way my mother was trying to "good advice" me into her world, when in reality I belonged in my own world. I felt like a squatter in hers.

When my daughter was born and had to be hospitalized, my mother came to town immediately. I did not have to be hospitalized—though I was still weak and a bit bloody, I was fine. The trouble was my girl's: she was having difficulty breathing and had to go on antibiotics. We were checked into St Luke's Hospital under her name, a name that (such a strange thought) had only existed for forty-eight hours. Of the things I had feared about her birth, not one single fear was that she would not be okay. Of course she would be okay. I feared pain, blood, being cut, tearing, being transferred, the length, the duration, the emotions, the pressure, but none of my fears were on her behalf. I had been thinking like a daughter.

My mother quit eating mammals after having children, something I did, too. I remember a moment when my father-in-law planned to shoot a sow and her piglets because, he said, "They breed like rabbits. Have you seen how big they get? They're the size of cars! They could kill us all." I found myself thinking that I couldn't blame them if they did, and it was a definite change in my alliances. I realized with an animal jolt that, however well we got along, I had much more in common with this sow than I did with my father-in-law.

Everything in my entire genealogy fought against leaving the daughter-only-camp—until a woman literally came out of me. Then, suddenly, I was climbing around the trees and could see the mastodons in the distance, and my very cells knew that my daughter was supposed to outlive me. It was a certainty, as was the heat of the sun, the wetness of water, the existence of dinosaurs.

Looking back on my mother as she must have been at my age, then back further, at my daughter's age, I feel a feral sort of love for her, and also a deep, maternal empathy. There is something so vulnerable about that young woman. Her home life fell apart; her father died when she was twenty-five, her stepmother took all the family money and tossed her childhood toys. She lost everything during her childhood—perhaps that is why she collects? Why gifts mean to her what they do?

6

At Madewell, my mother beelined to the counter, where laidback young women so unlike the two of us folded clothes into tissue paper for the hip clientele. My mother, the most intense person in the shop, and also by far the oldest, squared her shoulders high and asked to see a blazer being held under her name.

The young employee named Mirabel, a small woman with a face like a thin petal and a large mole on her forehead, checked. "Could it be under another name?" she asked.

I gave my name. Nothing. My mother's face and shoulders began to fall. This was a huge disappointment for her, and I could see she was not going to let it go. "How disappointing," my mother said to me, in a voice meant for Mirabel. "I used to think this was a great store."

Mirabel looked again, this time digging into a huge barrel of blue jeans, scattering them all over the floor.

No blazer. Then she asked, "Do you remember who said she'd reserve it for you? I could list the names."

My mother was out for revenge. Mirabel could tell. Whoever this Madewell employee was who had failed to hold the blazer was on my mama's shit-list, and she wanted her fired or at least in trouble. Mirabel listed a few women's names who were working last night. None seemed to ring a bell. But while Mirabel and I waited to see on which one my mother would pin the guilty act, Mirabel asked gently, "Would you like me to check in the back?"

My mother gave a terse nod.

While she and I waited, we looked around. This was definitely not my kind of store. My mother knew that. Neither of us are comfortable with silence, and she broke it first: "Last time I was here I saw a pair of really cute stovepipe pants that would look great on you. But I know they're not your style."

"I know."

She smiled. "I know you know I know."

7

One of my earliest memories of my mother is that she used to spread out a tarp in the living room on cold days and put a sandbox on it so that we could have a beach inside. My mother had a brood, four of us, all young at once. It would not have been easy for her to truck us all down to the park. A park within blocks, a nice park that children use, is a luxury—I think how my parents would've loved such a gift during my childhood. My daughter and I, on the nice days, always walked to the park. There is a swing she loved, a slide, and sand. One child is easy—you can walk to find sand.

The winter my daughter turned two, my mother sent me a sandbox.

Did she give me this gift anticipating more children and the impossibility of walks to the park? Or did she give it so that my daughter, like me, could have the great fun of playing with sand during the long northern winter months?

My daughter comes with me to cafes, on walks, and to dinners, where she hangs out with the crowd until she begins to rub her eyes, and then she goes to sleep in a Pack-and-Play in a back bedroom. She makes friends in a jiffy, like my mother and I do. She is portable. She travels light. She has a backpack she adores and she loves to put things in it. Her things. Things she chooses. Things of her own.

My mother's sandbox rested against the wall in our empty living room for a week.

The thought of filling it with water and sand, having my daughter use it for a week, then move on, filled me with dread. The thought of myself, not-writing, not-teaching, not-reading bedtime stories, not-making pancakes, not-parenting. Just cleaning up sand forever, and ever, and ever, and ever.

"You win some, you lose some," was the subject of the email my husband sent to my mom. "Elisabeth McKetta came into my office today crying about a sandbox. Ok if I give it to the school?"

My bountiful mother wrote back within the hour: "Thank you for letting me know . . . yes of course, give it to the school if they want it . . . sorry for any trouble that the gift caused."

We gave the sandbox to the Montessori school. They were excited to have it.

8

My mother knows that I only wear two things ever: simple (mostly black) knee-length dresses without zips, buttons, or patterns (with leggings and a sweater in the winter); and yoga pants with black t-shirts painted by my artist friend Troy with phrases like "poets are weirdos" or "breathe" or "egaruoc," which is courage backwards so you see it the right way in the mirror. I require very few clothes.

My mother also knows that I dislike all shopping except for food shopping. We both love shopping for food, because it feels productive, nourishing—it feeds our family. We both go to our local Whole Foods five to ten times a week on average, which we both know is absurd, yet somehow neither of us can help it. Like mother like daughter. My daughter loves clothes and really likes to shop for them, and even though I loathe clothing shopping, I need to remember to do it with her and have fun doing so. My mother and daughter, each time they are in the same town, make a trip to dress the girl for the year. My mother knows how much fun it is to buy things you know your daughter— and her daughter, and onward down the generations— will love.

I know this, too. Just the previous night, when I was at an opening for a Gabriel García Márquez exhibit just down the street from my parents' house, we were served Colombian food with doll-sized spoons and forks. My daughter is so deeply into her American Girl doll, Samantha, that she makes her a seat at every table and tears apart pieces of popcorn for her as an afternoon snack. Incidentally, her Samantha doll was a Christmas gift to me from my mother's mother, who died five months later. The doll was what I had wanted more than anything else, and my parents would not buy it because it was too expensive. But Nana, who lived frugally in an apartment and had me over weekly to make Rice Krispy treats, Nana who knew her time on earth was up soon, decided for my sake to splurge.

I was nine when I received the doll—my daughter's age as I write this. I loved that doll ferociously until I outgrew her, and then my mother boxed her and waited patiently for the next generation. When that time came, my mother had Samantha fixed up at the Doll Hospital, her legs reattached and her hair denested, to give her for Christmas to my daughter. A gift to a daughter's daughter, gifted to a daughter's daughter, thirty years apart. The gift itself, a sort of daughter: or at least that doll felt like a daughter to me.

Now she is like a daughter to my daughter.

At any rate: at the exhibit, I waited by the food bar and gathered a handful of these tiny forks and spoons so I could pack them in my bag and bring them home for my daughter's dolls. My husband would say, "Why are you hoarding this junk?" And he would be only partially right.

9

Mirabel returned. She had a gray blazer, XS, in a completely different style that neither my mom nor I liked. Mirabel knew this; she had tried her best.

"It's okay, Mom," I said. And at last I told the full truth: "I don't like it enough to warrant this. It's a nice blazer, but it's not necessary. Let's go home."

But my mother was like a knight on a quest, and there was no stopping her. "Elisabeth, please permit me," she said. Then back to Mirabel she turned.

Mirabel said, "We could see if there is an XS in gray in another store in the US, then we could ship it to you."

"Yes, let's do that," my mother said decisively.

"But if it doesn't fit," I said, "I won't have any way to return it."

"Just save it for me when I visit next," my mother said, her lips pursed like a general's, and she followed Mirabel up to the register. Mirabel called Headquarters. She was put on hold. Then she asked me for my address. I gave it to her, but she wrote my mother's name as the person living there. I pointed this out and gave her my name, and she changed it.

She misspelled my first name, and I could feel my mother wincing invisibly next to me.

At this point in Mirabel's series of agonizing efforts, my mother and I stared at each other. Was it a stalemate? Was it instinct, or genetic coding? Was my mother about to give up? It felt like we looked at each other so long that we folded into each other's reflections. So long that perhaps we are still there, still looking.

My mother is furious. I am near-panic-overwhelmed. This day could go one way, or it could go another. This is not the first time I have had a rift with my mother over a gift.

I turn away first.

This store has tiny travel kits and candles and expensive lotions and a thousand dresses I would never choose to wear. While we waited for Mirabel's next attempt, I looked at the lotions, noticing that the ingredients were many of the same oils and essential oils I had at home: castor oil, olive oil, lavender, cardamom, rose hip—but into those oils were mixed various chemical preservatives. Words that our grandmothers would not be able to pronounce.

I thought, I am so glad I make my own toiletries and cleansers and lotions. This stuff is just filler. The same could be said about just about everything.

My mom, waiting for Mirabel to place the order so she could give her credit card, said sensitively to me, "Do you want to look around at any other stores outside? I'll wait here."

This was a generous act of rescue; only she knew to what extent.

So I stood outside in the sunlight, at the edge of the parking area. A one-man band played Janis Joplin's "Bobby McGee," one of my favorite songs from high school. Beautiful South Austin women shuffled around, twirling down the sidewalks with their shopping bags. Across the street stood the ivy-covered hotel where my two non-family wedding guests had stayed for two nights. Down the street, I could see the iconic Austin motel sign shaped like a middle finger riding from the humped knuckles of a hand, or like an erect penis and testicles; it felt either angry or reproductive, depending on the viewer's mood.

I stretched and did some yoga in the sun. I thought, this is my mother. Persistent. Unable to let a thing go, especially when it involves her children. Whether advice or a blazer. No matter how long I live, I will never have her persistence.

But I have other qualities that are foreign to her. I am her daughter who needs next to nothing. My house where I live with husband and children is smaller than my mother's kitchen, and yet we have everything there we need. My mother at seventy-three still calls realtors regularly to try to buy a house big enough for all of her children, should they all at once ever want to come home.

10

The last time I'd had a meal with both my parents and my children had been at an elegant restaurant near my tiny house, several months earlier. I think it was Christmas Eve, or the eve before it. My daughter packed her doll Samantha for dinner, and her packing took a long time. I knew without a doubt that my parents were early to the restaurant, my mom reminding my dad to relax and stop checking the time. At home, my son, husband, and I stood in our restaurant clothes, my six-year-old son itching in his fancy wool pants and wiggling a tooth, talking about strings and doorknobs, while she packed Samantha's tiny doll backpack.

"There," my daughter pronounced. We made it to the car, my spouse grumbling about grandparents' gifts. We made it to dinner almost on time.

The meal was one of the best I can remember having with both my parents and my young: nobody checked their phones, everybody laughed, even the children were engaged in the storytelling.

Midway through the meal, my daughter turned to me. "I didn't even need Samantha's backpack. I didn't need any of her stuff. All I needed was her placemat,

her pickles, her granola bar, and her water-bottle. I
didn't even need her microphone."

11

Back at the store, my mom was nearly done paying for
the blazer, and she was thanking Mirabel and giving
her compliments. "I like your shirt," my mother was
saying. "Isn't it so pretty how it opens at the back?"

This was her way of connecting, of apologizing.

Then we walked out of Madewell, to our badly
parked car.

We got into the car, both looking ahead and not at
each other, fussing with our seatbelts, waiting for the
other to assess what we had just experienced, to label
it "good" or "bad" or "funny" in our shared lexicon of
values, our inborn, invisible mother-daughter encyclo-
pedia that blurred and slackened the longer we lived
apart.

"Elisabeth," she said, facing me directly at last, "you
are the most patient person I have ever met."

"Mom," I said, "you are the most persistent."

She went on: "I know you don't like clothes shopping. I like clothes shopping for YOU."

"I know," I said, thinking maybe one day I will like
doing it for my own daughter.

12

My mother taught me to fight chaos with chaos. As an
adult, I cannot. I fight it, fight to the bestial death, with
order.

I have worked hard to be rooted, to tamp down
the unruly parts, to outsource tasks to other people,
to take care of my children and my work and myself. I

have daily routines, independent children, a calendar, generally good boundaries, dependable friends.

When my mother comes to town, she works systematically and lovingly to uproot all of this.

I know you said she has to carry all her own luggage, but . . .

I know you only have a little bit of closet space at home, but . . .

I know you said the dog only eats one scoop of kibble, but . . .

My son is using the bathroom. "Does he need help wiping?" my mother asks. "But are you sure he can do it? He is only four!"

I remember once my daughter was frustrated because she tried to advise her brother on which jellybeans to eat that wouldn't taste like toothpaste or ginger, and he told her to go away. *He is asking for autonomy*, she and I concluded. But she remained wounded and indignant. Her preadolescent eyes are hard; they are a dark and watchful brown like mine, like my mother's, like her mother's. My daughter's eyes glare around the room like a judge at court. She has help to give, and how dare nobody want it! Like mother like grandmother, snaking all the way up the line.

13

The gray blazer arrives on my mother's birthday in early March.

"It looks nice," my husband says in a tone of surprise.

When the pandemic struck, I moved overnight to England with my family, packing, in a curious moment of anticipating winter and having no idea how long we'd stay, the gray woolen blazer. My parents fled their house and their red state to the next blue state over, though with a little more preparation. Like mother like daughter.

In the cold Cornish summer that is not a summer by any Texan standards, I wear that gray blazer that my mom gave me every . . . single . . . day. It is warm. It is comfortable. It lasted the summer and the fall and the winter and the spring. It still lasts, unlike many of the other clothes I brought that have since fallen apart. It is solid, warm, weighty, essential.

It is made well, as the company promises.

I suppose, in the end, so are we, my mother and I.

Basking

1

"Poor old thing."

This is what our neighbor Paul says as he looks down upon the shark.

It is late afternoon, and all of our hamlet neighbors have come tumbling down to the beach to look at a basking shark that has washed ashore and died. Paul, a young and gentle soul married to Petra the professor, is looking and looking at the big fish. We all are.

Guus, the Dutch underwater photographer partnered with Charlie, the free-diving yogi, thinks he saw the shark's mouth move and gently waves his hand over its eye to see if there is any awareness. None. We all know this is impossible, for its stomach has spilled out of its skin, puffing out like a small paper bag that hopeful children bring to school on holidays to carry home candy. And still we hope.

An hour from now, scientists from Trinity, Ireland will fly to our little hamlet to cut filets from the shark's spine and brain to test it for meningitis. One, a young woman in her twenties, will answer my children's questions amiably, wearing her rubber gloves and holding midair her knife. The following morning, the word will have spread, and children in their school uniforms will ask their parents to drive them down the beach to take a look before school.

When they are home, my babies want to talk about the shark. Death is interesting to the young, which is why I tell them so many fairy tales. My fast-growing babies, at six and ten, are lawless, godless, schoolless, countryless, and compared to their former lives, friendless. At least they have cardboard and each other.

They want to know about this lone shark. This juvenile. Washed up on the unlikeliest of beaches.

The other question they ask, but know we cannot answer, is about the house. For the house we landed in, our pandemic house, where we have been living in safety and ease, this house we hoped to buy and live in forever, is about to be bought out from under us.

In a hamlet this size—called a hamlet and not a village because it lacks a church—our fourteen neighbors have come to like us well enough. My husband thinks they will be sad to see us go; my son says seriously, "We are the village's *favorite* children." Our new friend Tony told him so. I will believe anything: four decades into being alive, I cannot count how many times I have loved easily and lost easily—I can believe that true love exists even without deep roots.

My husband heard one neighbor say to another neighbor: "All they did was fall in love, like the rest of us did, and try to find way to stay, like the rest of us have." We are pitied a bit, like most Americans these days. Like the shark.

2

When the virus got so bad in our state that we couldn't leave our house, and the armed anti-maskers were breaking windows at the capitol a mile away, my husband, two small children, and I left our dog with a friend and moved—through a combination of blind luck and good googling—here. To a sea-facing bungalow in a tiny fishing hamlet in Cornwall, England.

We arrived shocked and jetlagged, having taken one giant step into the air. We had fled our country as if it were a sinking ship, bought tickets on my birthday, packed our lives the following day, flown out the third. We didn't know if we would stay for six months or forever. Or something in between.

From the bungalow, the morning sun gleams on the white faces of the houses across the way. The ocean (blue) and the sky (pink) press together like stern, mismatched lips. Suddenly the weather changes, as it does many times a day. From our window to the north, we see our neighbors' cottages, piled like bright white pebbles upon the hill. Some of these neighbors are newer, like us, but most have lived here for seven generations; their fathers were quarry workers and their great-grandfathers built the long bungalow in which we live, which used to house miners. Below their homes, we see a dozen old boats scattered about on the gravel. We see the salted old red phone booth, too cobwebbed to enter, next to the flagpole with the torn Cornish flag. It looks like a pirate flag, my son observed. Just without the skull.

To the east, we see only the ocean. We quickly buy a telescope; it belongs more to the house than to us. My husband and my son spend their days looking out the window.

Later, my husband would say that we had had the best virustime ever, landed in a place where the sickness virtually didn't exist, and we had gone about our lives. Looking at him now, with his uncut smile and retired-dad hair, I think: perhaps this was his era. The one that divided his before and after. "It was a perfect nine months," he would later say.

The people who have lived here forever are used to it, but still they carry binoculars on their walks, for you never know what you might see in the sea. The newcomers call this place "Paradise." It is a paradise, for the newcomers, but it has the rubbery manufactured stench of inferno for the old families whose roots run so deep, but whose children will not be able to afford to stay. Family fishing is on the out, and their homes are becoming other people's second homes, sold for much more than they could pay to stay.

So maybe it is the land of lotus eaters. But then another poem from another country interrupts: "but miles to go before I sleep . . ."

When is it time to rest and settle? Are we living here, or just basking, for a time?

3

We have a three-year visa to stay in England that is based on my writing. Nightly, my husband and I pick through the sand to determine our next steps, starting with where we will live. We hold in our minds the possibilities of many lives: Will we stay here, and will the children spring from our arms into their own lives? Will we return to Boise, where we have such good friends, where the laws and driving and everything are familiar, flawed but at least our own? Could we live forever in the shadow of the Rocky Mountains, the lowest of their foothills taller than anything here? Could we live in the familiar shadows of the problems of our country, which long lay underwater like threatening sea creatures and are now coming up to bite?

We don't know. Both lives exist, and day by day we ebb and flow between them.

But it feels somehow holy, like prayer in my secular heart, to see this shark. It feels somehow like a forced remembering that we all risk dying alone and far from home. It feels elemental and somber, humble and rooted in the ordinary currents of life and death.

We had lost our hearts to this house, this beach, this hamlet.

"Sometimes our dreams outstrip our bank accounts," my dad said when he saw where this story was going. Still we dreamed on.

But each week more people came to tour the house, parking in Land Rovers—too big for these Cornish hedge-roads, their drivers refusing to back up or pull over or do any of the things that are customary here to make way for another car. In Cornwall, every car must sometimes drive in the hedge. What the Cornish say about the Land Rovers is that they are afraid to get scratched. "I hate that they're trying to steal our house," my husband says each time we have to clean up and make way for another tour.

But we, by being here, surely have stolen another's house, which they stole from another, and another, and another. Each new purchase, now, is a severance of deep roots that will end with this generation as England and the rest of the world comes here to buy.

A house is an innocent in the greed-games of humans. I know this. Still I want to pat the house, like a great horse, and tell it, *you are good*.

4

There is a feeling a writer gets upon completing an ambitious project that can only be described as basking. Champagne nearby is a plus. You are fully aware that more work is to come but not *this* work. You soften your peripheral vision. Look only just ahead. From where I stand now, what is just ahead and worth looking at is a hedge, green in springtime and waving in the wind. And daffodils. And in front of me, just down, a half-eaten Cornish pasty.

What are you doing here? I ask myself most days.

Basking. I suppose.

Supposing is not my forte. I want to know, with certainty, the plan. Now and forever. So this unknowing is mightily unnerving.

But it is good practice.

For what?

Not knowing.

5

We fall asleep to the news my husband reads aloud at night. America fighting about whether or not the election was rigged.

The news picks clean our year.

We wake to the morning scrawl of the birds. The whipping wind that everyone warned us about, but which we love. Today it woke me around five because it sounded like the ocean was lathering its hands.

We have been washed here, washed and weathered. I see the change in my face, in my husband's face.

This week, grading—the work that pays for our house here—is seemingly endless. This week, fifty-three papers between the two universities where I teach. Each of these is a piece of real writing by a real person, a real writer, and I must treat their writing with respect. I enjoy this, but during weeks like this I feel like my writing and my living soul get fractured into fifty-three slivers of apartment where other writers live. I am largely absent from my home, my own books, my attention slivered away from my babies. It is often on weeks such as these that I have time-consuming existential crises requiring treats, like pasties. I am delicate. Made of cartilage, not bone. One punch, and the nose collapses.

From the window, I see our friend Tony with his hands knotted behind his back and his perfectly trained dogs flanking him. There is life; here is writing. Today I decide in favor of life, and make coffee, and put on my tall mucker boots, and clomp across the stream below our house with two cups of coffee in hand to chat with Tony.

"This is just like you," he says in his voice from another country, another age, but full of the familiar language of laughter. "You splashing straight across, even if you get water in your boots. I can tell your husband is more careful. He balances you."

We talk about this year, about the contested election results in America. His wife has gotten the first virus jab, and Tony is happy about that.

"What a year," Tony says, and anyone on any side of any divide would have to agree.

I think, as I return to the house with our coffee cups on my fingers to continue my grading, that this year has been like a wave—turbulent at first, shaking everything into confusion, impossible to get on top of, rising, rising, but then ultimately gentle, rolling in, landing us here. In the end, didn't we all gain something? Despite all the loss, the past year reacquainted everyone with home.

Or perhaps 2020 is more like the shark, first under-water, unknown, sick—but at the end, it was calm, open-mouthed, and expansive. There you have it. 2020 as one big dead shark. Who knows what the year is. At some point I must give up on trying to solve the world using words.

Words, after all, are a home for the writer, but only one home. A writer always lives half in this world and half in the world she's writing about. To leap into unex-pected places is not such a task for the writer who is still half-living in some other story. She will always fol-low the magic, for the lightning-flash of time of being alive, almost as if she cannot help it. Life, after all, is only this tiny little island floating on top of eternity. A temporary home. A basking place. And, if we are lucky, a soft place to die.

6

Have we done it then? Have we broken through the meniscus of country? Have we pulled up our roots that far? My son is losing teeth at a rapid rate. They fall out of his mouth like seeds of corn. Like shark's teeth.

The one that stuck, he got tired of, and he actually did the shut-door trick. I had never imagined that people truly did this, especially not people that I made. He tapped closed our cottage kitchen door, and out it came. He grinned in his underwear and school uniform sweater.

I got dizzy and faint.

"Lie down on the floor!" my husband commanded. My son, now without any top front teeth, climbed up on the counter and made me a calming cup of black tea. I felt dizzy all day when I thought of the tooth. Pulled up like that from the roots.

The day before, my son had lost his shoe in the deep, black mud. It took an hour of poking the mud with a stick to find it. The day before the day before, my husband swam for six hours straight. The people watching him on Penzance shore said—no joke—that for part of his swim, a basking shark was swimming alongside him. "You could've reached out your arm and touched it!" He had not noticed. When he swims he looks straight down, alone, just himself. How do all these stories fit together?

What if we stayed in paradise? I think purgatory is where life lives. The place of disagreements. First and last suppers. Missing children's shoes. Did we skip out too soon? I prowl the house at night, thinking that perhaps paradise versus purgatory isn't the right question. Perhaps, right now, they are one and the same.

7

On our first night, jellyfish dot the gravel at low tide like little plastic cup tops, and we pick them up and toss them back. They are not the stinging sort. We walk away from the beach, past a seawall with rusting pipework that is peeling off from age and the mild salt in the wind, up the hill, to the opposite side of the working gravel quarry—up, up, past the settee rock where an old Cornish man with his herding dogs introduces himself as Tony and the rock as the Thinking Rock, where you can bring all your problems and leave them for the sea to solve.

Every day we go on a long green walk. The hedges hug the roads, and the trees arc over the roads like green cathedrals. We call them tree tunnels. With a year of no drivers, the hedges would surely swallow these tiny roads. The hedges are like tall salads to those who know foraging. I know three plants and nibble as I walk. The cars come fast, so we walk single-file and with care. We either walk to the sea or past the cows, which means to town. We pass tiny villages with bright gardens. Early in our stay, a woman named Sarah threw open her door when she saw us admiring her loom. She said, "You are the ones living at The Bungalow." She says it with certainty, then adds, "People are a bit nosy here!" We forget her name and apologize, and she scolds us vigorously. "People are like flowers," she says, forgiving us. "We worry so much about knowing their names, but all we should really do is enjoy them."

On the walks home from school my husband teaches our children to build dams on the little stream. On the walks to school I tell them fairy tales. Then I keep my walk home, two green solitary miles, for thinking, holding the thoughts in my head until the bursting point, like holding one's breath underwater, then let them out in a single long exhalation when I get home, wild words on a page.

This era, like the era of having very young children, is almost too beautiful to look at straight-on. You must appraise it sideways, while you are doing something else, for otherwise it will burst through the mind like water through a dam. There is just too much. Somehow, only in this way, you can bask in the memory, at least until it washes off.

We asked my parents for a loan to buy the house. It was the only time I ever asked my parents for money. They had offered it often, and I had tried always to live in a way that I could refuse. But when I asked in 2020, at age forty-one, they said no. I didn't blame them. It was an expensive dream.

When I was beating my head about the house, thinking if there was anything I hadn't yet thought of, Tony saw me kicking the kids' turquoise soccer ball, and called out: "Training for the nationals?" Then he invited us for tea.

When we are gone, after these conversations fade, will I remember the green aliveness of this place? I cannot overstate the GREEN. The pale green out my desk window, all around the white, pink, and blue clustering hydrangeas. Then the deep chlorophyll green of the forest, the moss overgrowing the stones on either side, and the messy twiggy green of each hedge, then the short-mowed green of the farmer's grasses. Dark green trees, light green field around the stream. Then the ocean and sky, about the same color many mornings: pale porpoise-blue.

In the modern world, says my husband, what do we gain?

8

In one week, two unrelated events: my mother had a hysterectomy, and the house we were living in went into a bidding war between two emmet couples—Cornish for "ants," meaning rich tourists from upcountry. We could not afford to stay in the bidding, not for a day. At one point, not so long before, when no buyers were biting and it was just us, we had thought we were the chosen buyers. We were right for it and it for us, the owner wrote in an email. He sent us old photos of the hamlet from the past century and a half, before the stone wall was built, when the beach was short and there was no football field, and we responded with enthusiasm. Now we were the guardians of the house who had to clean it twice a week so that couples with deep pockets could come and offer more than whatever the current offer was, so the house could become a gold mine for the owner who had built the addition to the humble miners' lodging.

That whole week, I thought of the walnut-sized room being taken out of my mother. I thought of the tiny house we had lived in so happily back in America, and I grieved what had happened to my city that made us wish to leave it. The guns, increasing and increasing. The Nazis my husband keeps dreaming about. They deface the Anne Frank statue again and again with graffiti and signs saying *we are everywhere*. I believe them. The angry citizens who tear down Black Lives Matter signs. Who show up at city councilmembers' houses with air-horns to protest masks. Who caused one councilwoman to run, crying, out of a meeting and home to her son, who was there alone being harassed and frightened by citizens who were angry at his mother. I thought of home and how once we leave it, we can never go back. It is never the same home and we are never the same dweller.

I mooned around the long white mining house. I craved Cornish pasties.

"Finish your grading and you'll feel better," my husband suggested. He was correct.

I thought of my husband and son, rooted by the ocean—I will remember each of them here, looking out the window through the telescope at boats.

"What roots you?" a Dutch friend once asked me, in her gentle way. She had left her village "where the grandmothers were" to go on an adventure in America with her husband. They had three children along the way. When she went back to the Netherlands she missed her villages in America, "where people seem so willing to be themselves." But, she said, in her home village, "I don't have to explain myself to anyone." Now she lives in neither: she lives in her husband's old village, where she is a wife imported and still without roots. I know this kind of wife: I have been her. My friend is training to be a naturopathic doctor, so she can be of use. When I was that imported, rootless wife, I trained myself to be a writer—and when I look back on my ten years in Boise, I see that writing was my home: it brought me to a life that turned out to be such rich soil, so nutrient-dense.

"Writing roots me," I told my friend automatically. "Writing and my family."

"But outside of your work?" she insists. "Are there other things that just feel good to you?"

Cities are the invisible answer. Walking in anonymity through endless city streets like a great labyrinth. Then why the hell did I lose my heart to this hamlet?

Because of the basking shark. Because of the daily embrace of wearing my mother's wool blazer, summer and winter and spring. Because of the ocean. Because of the hedges full of green everything. Because of this long, beautiful, elevated mother-home. Because I like to watch my people look out the windows.

9

Each time in my life so far, when I was given a choice between money and time, adult respectability and giddy childish love, I chose the freer seeming one: always the second. Autonomy: a word my children know and love. Perhaps that desire for autonomy did catapult us here—out of the home of the free, and here. Free to be in a very old part of a very old country, where cows and sheep graze, and where sharks sometimes come to die.

It's not time for me to retire yet, not time to think about dying, yet here at the ocean both possibilities feel very much alive. And it is comforting somehow to watch those possibilities playing together like children on the beach. So perhaps this is a goodbye to that young adulthood. A swan song. Or is it a shark song?

When Tony, who had lived nearly eighty years with the certainty that he would die within a few miles of where he was born, saw the shark, he said, "I've seen a lot of friends die in the war; dying is one thing, dying alone is another. And that poor old thing died alone on strange shores."

10

My once brand-new husband had owned a house in Boise for four years already when I arrived. I felt a bit like Bluebeard's wife journeying through the woods to pop up in this new village. *Hello!* she says, unsuspecting. A wife imported and still without roots.

Though the fairy tale analogy ends there, there was truth to the feeling that the city where we first lived had a currency of its own—mountain biking, white-water kayaking, camping—and being someone who mostly read and wrote didn't seem to have much social use. But writers find their pack, and I threw my hat into any writerly thing I heard whisper of, and by the year's end I had two writing groups, a book club, and a community of slam storytellers, as well as a new moth-ers' group (my daughter was born six months into this venture).

We were all new in town, seeking better lives for ourselves and our young. Sometimes it seems like a city in a certain era—Paris in the 1920s, Hollywood in the 1930s, Detroit in the 1950s, Austin in the 1980s—has an expiration date. In the early 2000s, Boise seemed a perfect city. Artists flourished. Good houses were cheap. Everyone knew each other. All the dogs got along. There was no traffic and people biked. Neigh-borhoods had block parties on summer nights. Life changes in any city. We left in 2020 when it started to change in ours.

I thought of another question my Dutch friend asked, hesitantly, about where in America we have our villages. "Everyone goes away," I told her. "Each gener-ation gets priced out."

I remember when my first nest thrust me out: when Austin suddenly swelled and outstripped what any new adult, facing the great google of one's twenties and seek-ing home, could buy into with a flimsy, hard-earned college degree and what the Brits call a "uni job." I remember living there, leaving for school, and wish-ing the impossible wish that I could go back to it: to when it smelled like wet trees and the cafes were small and filled with friends, and the downtown was empty at night. To before, when all our stay-at-home moms and sweet working dads could afford lovely houses in central neighborhoods. Now those homes are reserved for people other than us, people other than our parents at our age, people other than our children when they stand on the cusp of their own adulthoods.

I was born to parents who were not rich but not poor, and we lived in a sweet, safe neighborhood of modest-sized houses that by my adulthood would sell for well over a million dollars each. My childhood friends and I had to choose between living on the outskirts of our city, in the lonely reaches beyond the highways where tow truck lots lurk behind razor fences, or living in tiny apartments near our old homes—either one a demotion—or leaving.

I left. I started a life in a sweet, safe neighborhood two thousand miles away, with families like mine (not rich and not poor) who were raising their children there. And when our children are grown, that neighborhood will be out of their reach. Already the Californians (like my husband) and Texans (like me) have come and driven the prices up. Our children will either accept a demotion in the city of their childhood, or they will go create a new village with new friends somewhere else. Sometimes their parents retire and join them and they recreate the pattern of the generations in one place. Then the new children grow up and must find a new village, the grandparents die, and the parents retire and move to where their children are. This migration of home is happening all over the world.

"There is no home," I told my Dutch friend. "No village in America. Not for most people."

"Then you must be like an air-plant," she observed. "Drawing your nutrients from the air and the people around you."

11

I have fallen in love before just as rashly, though I don't think my husband has, even for me: his love is more careful. He spends time in the calculation of costs/benefits, a sort of pro forma of the heart. He does this for every house we look at once it becomes certain we cannot keep this one.

But I loved him simply and without question when we met. I loved him when I thought we were going to run out of money and when both of our children were born. I loved him when he got bitten by a bat and we both thought he might die. I loved him when we both lost our tempers and I said the meanest things I could think to say, and when he said equally hateful things back that landed like ninja stars in my pregnant belly. We had done numbers on each other, as all marrieds do. We were amputees. Now we love each other with a calm love, no longer just juvenile. He brings the ocean everywhere, swims channels between islands for fun, makes me think of sea lions, sea foam, a mouthful of the loin of some delicate fish.

I love, in no particular order, how he talks at night when I am feeling quiet; how he trusts entirely his body and its limits; how he plays the ukulele when he is happy to be near water; how he sees all projects democratically, and puts equally as much investment into making cookies as finding us a house as teaching the children forgiveness; how he makes a good family shell, at whose edges I constantly push; how he gets up in the night for our children when they are sick or afraid; how unafraid of bodies he is; how he picks up crabs and holds them for children to see; and I love how, when I lamented having no exact role model for the precise life I wished to live, he bravely said, "You must be your own."

Once, in another decade and another ocean, we explored an island at night; it was guarded by a large male seal, and we rowed past him. It was the bravest thing I had ever done. When we got back, and my hair wouldn't dry, and I couldn't stop trembling and there was sand in our bed, I thought: *I have been so brave for you.* That night, I inexplicably forgave every past discord. I had soaked his salt water into my hardy long roots and survived. In that full moon night, I knew: This man keeps my thoughts above water.

We are not religious. We believe we get each other for this life and that's all.

A younger writer asked me for advice. I told him: choose as your partner someone who is not afraid of the world.

12

We have an Easterly blowing in. The shark is still down there, cut up, and will be either washed away or buried by tomorrow. Poor old thing.

I told my Dutch friend about it, and she said it sounds like a metaphor for 2020. I told her I had thought the very same thing.

I have been thinking about the shark. How it felt to see it washed up on our beach on the day we were looking at properties on other beaches. How the village all came down, and how we all felt something together. I am thinking about it also as a metaphor, though I'm not sure yet for what. I wake to find a lump where it has been buried in beach gravel, where it may stay forever and decompose beneath the daily activities of the holidaymakers and those who live here.

Someone else will come look at the house on Friday, before the bidding war closes. Even if our wish is dying, our wish is nearly done, this feels like one more variable, after everything we have already surpassed, nearly or possibly. First, we got a visa. Then, we got a loan. Then we met the owner, and it seemed that he liked us. We thought we had cleared all the hurdles. And then the early Christmas buyers came.

We have a Christmas tree here, bought from the neighboring farm. It is decorated fully with kids' art, mostly paper, popsicle sticks, and pipe cleaners. We stand it between the kitchen and the ocean. Christmas morning, we meet our neighbors for a cold dip at the beach. All Christmas afternoon, my husband looks at the ocean with his telescope and my son leans out the window, looking at the village. My window-looking men.

We are looking at other houses.

Come the end of our lease, we will not be a rural family after all. We will go on to find a balance between this green haven and an ordinary city where people work and shop and drive. A place, and a love, more familiar to us than this. It will suit us in a post-virustime world. But still it feels like a loss.

Losing Paradise feels like a gift we'd been given is being returned too soon. This finding footing and then finding it again, this endless balancing between what we lose our hearts to and what the constraints of life require—between love and compromise—in other words, adulthood.

13

Our neighbors have given us fish, cabbages, fudge, books, icebox cake, saffron buns, and toys. My husband does some research and learns how to make perfect American chocolate-chip cookies, and several times a month he sends the children with cookies for all the neighbors. They are very good cookies, and Alexander who owns the Food Hub suggests he make a shop here, or wherever we land.

Before we left, we took one of Alexander's cabbages and a huge cauldron of a pot, and I made a soup called schchi, a Ukrainian peasant soup. I made a lot of it and brought it in bags to the villagers.

"My soup fairy!" Minnie the shop-owner said. "I have been waiting all my life for this."

Tony looked grim and apologized. "My wife is on a strict diet, see, and won't be able to eat it; if I bring it home she'll stay awake all night worrying you won't like her. Sorry, darling, but you're my friend and friends deserve the truth."

I retrieved the soup and said not to feel bad. I told him my belief that some gifts you receive aren't for you to keep—they're just for the giving.

Before we left, my son turned the old red phone booth into a shell shop, then my daughter brought in vases of flowers. It was shiny and clean when we left, but knowing how everything by the ocean soon gets salted and wet and mossed over, I doubt it is in good shape now. It is buried by the weather and spores, dusted over. Something the beach-goers will ignore but the villagers will remember. Something that once existed.

14

Well, I thought when the virus struck, *here's goodbye to friends, cafes, and monthly massages.*

But then I found I had something else: Patience. Endless, bountiful patience. Glacial patience.

I want everybody in my village, however big or small, to be happy—even if it takes a long time, even if we have to drift around all the ports in the whole periplus of the world until we find our right landing place. I accidentally start a conversation that hurts my husband's feelings and I apologize for three days. (Three days, he at last pointed out, when I should've been grading.)

I tell my students at the end of term that there are only three stories: birth, love, death. Again and again. We left the city of my children's childhood—death— to leap to another country—birth—where we cultivated a dream specific to its contours and its offerings and its beauty—love. Then our dream evaporated with the selling of this house—death, again. There will be another birth, I just don't know what.

Keep writing, I tell myself. My children know this instinctively. They play and play, building cardboard hotels and dwellings and free gift stands—"honesty boxes," as they call them here—for their toys. My husband, too: he bakes cookies for the neighbors, runs out of butter, rushes to Tesco on Christmas Eve morning, bakes some more. What else are we to do?

15

Where will you wash up? our neighbors wonder. We wonder, too. We are in a short-term rental that will lead to another short-term rental, to another—and onward, like the discs of a spine.

"Will there be magic there, too, like there is here?" my son asks.

"Oh yes," I hear my daughter tell him. "Because we bring the magic."

My cellular walls between I and we have thinned. They have gone from bone to cartilage to nothing. When my mother asks, I can tell her the truth: I have not craved solitude. I have gotten enough nourishment from the world around me, from the world of my others.

I love love love love love you, my son says.

I love love love love love you, I say back.

You are the best mom in the entire world.

You are the best son in the entire world.

We are both telling the truth.

This sudden feeling of bounty, of patience, is everywhere, a whole mine of it beneath my feet: like petroleum seeping up from the ocean floor, like the generous legacy of a thousand thousand lost dinosaurs, the bounty this reduction in life brings is everywhere. I am drunk with it, I am basking in it, I want it to last forever. The loss of something in the past has been the present's tremendous gain. The world has snapped shut, and we have only us.

16

Our final night in Paradise a magnificent thunderstorm shakes the windows and skylights of this ocean house.

Just before we go to bed, all the wild winds stop and the full February cold moon rises over the ocean, casting its light on the water below: a luminous sea-path that looks almost as if we could walk on it to the end of the world. We stop everything and look, even the kids. It is lucky we do, for moments later the darkening clouds come again, blotting out the moon and leaving only us, standing in the darkness next to borrowed furniture and our dying Christmas tree.

What if, I think, we could move into the little cottage up the road, through whose windows you can see endless pastures, cows, sheep, and rabbits, and from whose uppermost corner in the attic room you can see a triangle of the moving ocean. It would be like a palindrome. Humble house that just fits us, with a shed in the back. To grandest house in the village. To humblest house, shorter in length, in fact, than a full-grown basking shark; to grandest house in a different village; to humble house that just fits us, with a shed in the back. Where we live happily ever after.

17

Once upon a time, there was a shark. It washed up dead in paradise. Now it is covered beneath the gravel beach. There it will stay buried, decomposing into memory, beneath the sands of everybody's vacation. Just like this year—this era, this house, these nine months imagining the next sixty years. Sanded over. But once open-mouthed, swimming, and very much alive.

Acknowledgments

THANKS TO ALL at Paul Dry Books, especially Julia, who sees what every piece of writing can be; Mara, who connects books to the world; and Paul, who started it all by reading the title essay and seeing its possibilities; and Ian, whose covers are pure magic. Thank you always to Lynn Miller, who for two decades has been my first reader. I spend my days in deep gratitude to the late Hope Hale Davis (1903–2004), who first read my journal entries and found something true; and thanks also to her daughter, Lydia Davis, for kindness, encouragement, and sending a dirndl. Thanks to Nancy Sommers, brave friend to all writers and beloved mentor to me. Thanks to my students worldwide in my Mythic Memoir course and all of my courses; your writings and your questions are always a source of inspiration. Thank you to Jona Klijn, for encouraging me to write what became "Basking," and for the gift of the line: "a soft place to die." Most of all, thank you each and every day to my entire family (born, married into, and made) for supporting this writer with love.

And thanks to the following who first featured earlier versions of some of these essays:

Bosque Journal: "Awake with Asashoryu"
Dare to be Fabulous (Borderlands, 2022): "Moist"
District Lit: "The Softness of Spikes"
Story Story Night: "The Scream," "Moist"
The Oxonian Review: "Toil"
What Doesn't Kill Her: A Collective Memoir (H&S Books, 2021): "Robber Face"